ECONOMIC ISSUES, PROBLEMS AND PERSPECTIVES

THE BUDGET CONTROL ACT OF 2011

ELEMENTS AND OPTIONS

ECONOMIC ISSUES, PROBLEMS AND PERSPECTIVES

Additional books in this series can be found on Nova's website under the Series tab.

Additional E-books in this series can be found on Nova's website under the E-book tab.

AMERICA IN THE 21ST CENTURY: POLITICAL AND ECONOMIC ISSUES

Additional books in this series can be found on Nova's website under the Series tab.

Additional E-books in this series can be found on Nova's website under the E-book tab.

ECONOMIC ISSUES, PROBLEMS AND PERSPECTIVES

THE BUDGET CONTROL ACT OF 2011

ELEMENTS AND OPTIONS

CHRISTOPHER G. LYNCH
AND
CORY MCHALE
EDITORS

Nova Science Publishers, Inc.
New York

For permission to use material from this book please contact us:
Telephone 631-231-7269; Fax 631-231-8175
Web Site: http://www.novapublishers.com

LIBRARY OF CONGRESS CATALOGING-IN-PUBLICATION DATA

The Budget Control Act of 2011 / editors, Christopher G. Lynch and Cory McHale.
p. cm.
Includes index.
CRS report for Congress prepared for members and committees of Congress.
ISBN 978-1-61942-035-9 (hardcover)
1. United States. Budget Control Act of 2011. 2. Budget--Law and legislation--United States. 3. Budget deficits $z United States. 4. Government spending policy $z United States. I. Lynch, Christopher G. II. McHale, Cory.
KF6225.Z9B83 2011
343.73'034--dc23

2011042425

Published by Nova Science Publishers, Inc. † New York

CONTENTS

PREFACE

The Budget Control Act (BCA) is the result of negotiations between the President and Congress held in response to the federal government having nearly reached its borrowing capacity. The BCA authorized increases in the debt limit of at least $2.1 trillion dollars (and up to $2.4 trillion under certain conditions), subject to a disapproval process that would likely require securing the support of two-thirds of each chamber to prevent a debt limit increase. It established caps on the amount of money that could be spent through the annual appropriations process for the next 10 years, which the CBO estimates will reduce federal spending by $917 billion. This book provides an overview of the essential features of the Budget Control Act, a history and recent increases of the debt limit and the potential effects on government operations.

Chapter 1 - The Budget Control Act (BCA) is the result of negotiations between the President and Congress held in response to the federal government having nearly reached its borrowing capacity.

The BCA authorized increases in the debt limit of at least $2.1 trillion dollars (and up to $2.4 trillion under certain conditions), subject to a disapproval process that would likely require securing the support of two-thirds of each chamber to prevent a debt limit increase. It established caps on the amount of money that could be spent through the annual appropriations process for the next 10 years, which the Congressional Budget Office (CBO) estimates will reduce federal spending by $917 billion. The BCA also created a Joint Select Committee on Deficit Reduction that is instructed to develop a bill to reduce the federal deficit by at least another $1.5 trillion over the 10 year period ending in FY2021.

Chapter 2 - If appropriations in the next 10 years are equal to the caps on discretionary spending and the maximum amount of funding is provided for the program integrity initiatives, CBO estimates that the legislation—apart from the provisions related to the joint select committee—would reduce budget deficits by $917 billion between 2012 and 2021. In addition, legislation originating with the joint select committee, or the automatic reductions in spending that would occur in the absence of such legislation, would reduce deficits by at least $1.2 trillion over the 10-year period. Therefore, the deficit reduction stemming from this legislation would total at least $2.1 trillion over the 2012-202 1 period.

Chapter 3 - Total federal debt can increase in two ways. First, debt increases when the government sells debt to the public to finance budget deficits and acquire the financial resources needed to meet its obligations. This increases *debt held by the public*. Second, debt increases when the federal government issues debt to certain government accounts, such as the Social Security, Medicare, and Transportation trust funds, in exchange for their reported surpluses. This increases *debt held by government accounts*. The sum of *debt held by the public* and *debt held by government accounts* is the total federal debt. Surpluses reduce debt held by the public, while deficits raise it. Treasury Secretary Timothy Geithner announced that the federal debt reached its statutory limit on May 16, 2011 and declared a debt issuance suspension period, allowing certain extraordinary measures to extend Treasury's borrowing capacity until early August 2011. Since May 16, debt subject to limit has hovered just below $14,294 billion. On August 2, 2011, President Obama signed into law the Budget Control Act of 2011 (S. 365), which included numerous provisions aimed at deficit reduction and an increase in the debt limit of up to $2,400 billion that would occur in several stages.

Chapter 4 - The gross federal debt, which represents the federal government's total outstanding debt, consists of two types of debt: (1) debt held by the public and (2) debt held in government accounts, also known as intragovernmental debt. Federal government borrowing increases for two primary reasons: (1) budget deficits and (2) investments of any federal government account surpluses in Treasury securities, as required by law. Nearly all of this debt is subject to the statutory limit. The federal debt limit currently stands at $14,294 billion.

In: The Budget Control Act of 2011
Editors: C. G. Lynch and C. McHale
ISBN: 978-1-61942-035-9

Chapter 1

THE BUDGET CONTROL ACT OF 2011*

Bill Heniff Jr., Elizabeth Rybicki and Shannon M. Mahan

SUMMARY

The Budget Control Act (BCA) is the result of negotiations between the President and Congress held in response to the federal government having nearly reached its borrowing capacity.

The BCA authorized increases in the debt limit of at least $2.1 trillion dollars (and up to $2.4 trillion under certain conditions), subject to a disapproval process that would likely require securing the support of two-thirds of each chamber to prevent a debt limit increase. It established caps on the amount of money that could be spent through the annual appropriations process for the next 10 years, which the Congressional Budget Office (CBO) estimates will reduce federal spending by $917 billion. The BCA also created a Joint Select Committee on Deficit Reduction that is instructed to develop a bill to reduce the federal deficit by at least another $1.5 trillion over the 10 year period ending in FY2021.

The legislation resulting from the joint committee recommendations can be considered under special procedures that prevent amendment and limit debate in both chambers. These procedures could have a significant impact in the Senate because they allow the bill to advance with simple majority support; under regular Senate procedures it can be necessary to

---

* This is an edited, reformatted and augmented version of a Congressional Research Service publication, CRS Report for Congress R41965, from www.crs.gov, dated August 19, 2011.

obtain agreement among at least three-fifths of the Senate (normally 60 Senators) to advance consideration of legislation.

If a joint committee proposal cutting the deficit by at least $1.2 trillion is not enacted by January 15, 2012, then the BCA established an automatic spending reduction process that includes sequestration (the cancellation of budgetary resources). The process presumably is intended to encourage agreement on deficit reduction, either by enacting the joint committee legislation by early 2012, or possibly by enacting other legislation (presumably through existing congressional procedures) by the beginning of 2013, when the automatic process would make reductions. If the enacted bill cuts the deficit by more than $1.2 trillion, an additional increase in the debt limit becomes available in the amount of the excess, up to $0.3 trillion.

The Budget Control Act has two additional elements. First, it directs that the House and Senate must each vote on a proposal to amend the Constitution to require that the budget of the federal government be balanced. The BCA does not alter the procedures for taking up such a measure in the Senate, and therefore the Senate might not be able to vote on passage of a constitutional amendment unless the support of 60 Senators can be secured to begin consideration. The only procedural consequence of not voting specified in the BCA is that, if Congress does not approve a constitutional amendment, the second of two conditions under which the act would permit an additional increase of $0.3 trillion in the debt ceiling, will not be available.

Second, the BCA also makes changes to the William D. Ford Federal Direct Loan (DL) program and the Federal Pell Grant program, two federal student aid programs authorized under Title IV of the Higher Education Act of 1965, as amended (HEA; P.L. 89-329). Effective July 1, 2012, the BCA eliminates the availability of Subsidized Stafford Loans to graduate and professional students and eliminates all but one type of repayment incentives on future DL program loans. CBO estimates these changes would reduce direct spending by $21.6 billion over the FY2012-FY2021 period. Approximately $17 billion of the $21.6 billion in estimated savings from the changes in the DL program would be directed to the Pell Grant program for future general use in FY2012 and FY2013.

INTRODUCTION

The President signed the Budget Control Act of 2011 (BCA; P.L. 112-25) on August 2, 2011. The new law contains multiple interrelated components, several of which establish procedures that will affect the consideration of subsequent legislation.

This report begins with a brief overview of the essential features of the Budget Control Act, taking a broad view of the connections between its different components and introducing readers to some fundamental concepts and terminology. The subsequent sections of this report provide more detailed information on each component of the BCA, with the goal of providing information to assist Members and staff as they apply these new procedures. (The appendices contain tools for those quickly seeking specific information: a list of short answers to "frequently asked questions" and tables identifying the various dates for action in relation to the bill to be proposed by the Joint Select Committee on Deficit Reduction and the resolutions disapproving the debt limit increase.)

The explanations of the procedures established in the BCA are based on a reading of the new law and an understanding of how similar procedures operated in the past. Some elements of the Budget Control Act of 2011, like all laws, will be subject to interpretation. Ultimately it is the House and Senate that will decide on the specific operation of the legislative procedures. For advice on the implementation of these procedures, congressional Members and staff will be best advised to consult with the Parliamentarian of their chamber. If an automatic spending reduction process is triggered, its actual execution will depend in large part on the interpretations and actions of the Office of Management and Budget (OMB), which might also need to be consulted regarding specific elements of that process.

BRIEF OVERVIEW OF ESSENTIAL FEATURES

Debt Ceiling Increase and Disapproval Process

The Budget Control Act is the result of negotiations between the President and Congress held in response to the federal government having nearly reached its borrowing capacity.[1]

The BCA authorized debt limit increases up to at least $2.1 trillion dollars (and up to $2.4 trillion under certain conditions) in three installments. The first installment of $400 billion already occurred when the President submitted a certification, pursuant to the act, that the debt was within $100 billion of its limit.[2] Congress can prevent each of the next two installments if it passes a joint resolution disapproving the increase to the debt limit and overrides an expected presidential veto, although this full sequence of actions is widely considered to be unlikely.

The initial passage of a resolution disapproving a debt limit increase requires majority support in each chamber; BCA procedures prevent a Senate filibuster that otherwise could delay or prevent its coming to a vote. Presumably, however, the President will veto the disapproval resolution because the Treasury will have advised him that further borrowing is required to meet existing commitments. To override a Presidential veto requires the support of two-thirds of both chambers. Ultimately, therefore, the support of two-thirds of each chamber might be necessary to prevent a debt limit increase.

The House and Senate might consider a resolution disapproving the next increase of $500 billion to the debt limit sometime in September, which is when the deadline set by the BCA for enacting such a resolution occurs. The debt is next predicted to be within $100 billion of its limit in early 2012, when the President would submit another certification and Congress might consider another disapproval resolution.

Statutory Discretionary Spending Limits

Reaching agreement on the debt ceiling increase contained in the BCA depended in part on enacting procedures designed to reduce future federal spending. The BCA therefore also established caps on the amount of money that could be spent through the annual appropriations process for the next 10 years, which the Congressional Budget Office estimates will reduce federal spending by $917 billion.[3] The caps established by the BCA may also be adjusted for certain purposes, including, for example, for the costs of the "Global War on Terrorism."[4]

The adjustable caps are not placed on specific accounts or even on each of the appropriations bills; instead they are broad caps on the total amount of discretionary spending. For the first two fiscal years, the caps are on two categories of spending: security and nonsecurity. For the other years, one limit on all discretionary spending is created. Decisions about how these caps will affect specific agencies or programs will be made by Congress and the President through the regular appropriations process.

Discretionary spending limits are not unique; in current practice, the appropriators generally operate under caps set by Congress in a budget resolution or in another form. But those caps are enforced in the House and Senate, and the House and Senate can each waive them unilaterally. The caps established by the BCA, in contrast, cannot be waived by a single chamber. If the caps are exceeded, the BCA provides for a sequestration process: an automatic, largely across-the-board cancellation of budgetary resources.

Joint Select Committee on Deficit Reduction

Another part of the BCA agreement to increase the debt ceiling was the creation of a Joint Select Committee on Deficit Reduction, instructed to develop legislation to reduce the federal deficit by at least another $1.5 trillion over the 10-year period ending in FY2021. The legislation resulting from the joint committee recommendations can be considered under special procedures that prevent amendment and limit debate in both chambers. These procedures could have a significant impact in the Senate because they allow a simple majority to approve a bill without indefinite delay. Under regular Senate procedures, the support of 60 Senators is often necessary to advance the consideration of legislation.

The joint committee, made up of an equal number of Democrats and Republicans from each chamber, has wide authority to develop a proposal to reduce the federal deficit. No specific policy restrictions or requirements are placed on the joint committee. Under the terms of the BCA it could recommend changes to revenue, spending, or both; it might even propose new budget enforcement mechanisms. For the proposal to be considered under the special, expedited procedures, however, it must be approved by the joint committee by November 23, 2011, and passed by both chambers by December 23, 2011. Given this timeline, perhaps the greatest indirect restriction on the content of the joint committee bill is that it must pass a House controlled by one party and a Senate controlled by another.

Budget Goal Enforcement: Spending Reduction Trigger

Furthermore, if Congress and the President do not enact a joint committee bill reducing the deficit by at least $1.2 trillion over the period of FY2012 to FY2021, there are potentially undesirable consequences. The failure to enact such a bill into law by January 15, 2012, will trigger an automatic spending reduction process. This process, sometimes referred to as "the trigger," includes sequestration, or the cancellation of budgetary resources. What it could mean is that if a qualifying joint committee bill is not enacted by

January 15, 2012, then on January 2, 2013, the spending authority of many federal departments and agencies will be reduced.

The automatic process for deficit reduction involves several steps and calculations, and for details the reader is referred to the "Budget Goal Enforcement" section of the report below. Very generally, the spending reductions are to be made equally from defense spending and from all other spending (referred to as "nondefense spending"). The reductions required in each of these categories are then divided proportionally between discretionary spending and mandatory spending.

The spending reductions are achieved for direct spending through sequestration each year (FY2013 to FY2021). For discretionary spending, the reductions are achieved through sequestration the first year (FY2013). For the other fiscal years (FY2014-FY2021), the discretionary spending reductions are achieved through a downward adjustment of statutory limits on discretionary spending divided into two new categories that reflect defense and nondefense spending. Importantly, some programs, including both Social Security and Medicaid, are exempt from sequestration, and any sequestration of Medicare spending is capped at 2%.

The precise implications of the automatic spending reduction process cannot be assessed at this time. The amounts of spending reductions required each year cannot yet be known, as they depend in part on the extent, if any, by which the reductions in the joint committee bill fall short of the $1.2 trillion goal and in part on spending estimates to be calculated in the future by the Office of Management and Budget (OMB). Furthermore, beginning in FY2014, part of the spending reductions will be achieved through a downward adjustment of the statutory limits on discretionary spending, not by automatic across-the-board spending cuts. For discretionary spending, it will therefore be Congress and the President who later determine the manner in which reductions are made to each account through the annual appropriations process each year.

This process presumably is intended to encourage agreement among policy makers on deficit reduction. During the negotiations over the BCA, it was widely reported that part of the reason to include both defense and domestic spending in the automatic spending reduction process was to encourage lawmakers to work to an agreement on deficit reduction based on an explicit determination of government budget priorities.[5] Presumably, such an agreement would be preferred by lawmakers to a largely across-the-board cut, proportional to each category, as described here. Thus, many lawmakers presumably have an incentive to prevent the automatic spending reduction process by enacting a joint committee bill reducing the deficit by $1.2 trillion or more over FY2012-FY2021. Congress and the President could also modify or terminate the process by passing a law altering the BCA, perhaps as part of the deal reached by the joint committee or perhaps in another law enacted sometime in 2012—because sequestration and other automatic spending reduction actions will not take place until 2013.

Vote on Constitutional Amendment to Balance the Budget

The BCA also states that the House and Senate must each vote on a balanced budget amendment to the Constitution between September 30 and December 31, 2011.[6] In the Senate, to get to a direct passage vote on a constitutional amendment, it might be necessary to secure support from 60 Senators to begin consideration of such a proposal. Many factors, including expectations created by approval of the BCA, could potentially influence whether or not the Senate votes on a balanced budget amendment. The only procedural consequence of not voting as specified in the BCA is that, if Congress does not *approve* a constitutional amendment, one of two avenues for increasing the debt ceiling by $1.5 trillion, instead of $1.2 trillion, will not be available.

If a joint resolution proposing a balanced budget amendment to the Constitution is approved by either chamber, then the BCA provides an expedited procedure for that joint resolution to be considered, without amendment, in the other chamber. The BCA does not affect procedures for bringing a measure up before the Senate, however. To summarize, if the House passes a balanced budget amendment by the required two-thirds vote, and if the Senate agrees to take up the House-passed proposal using its regular procedures, then the BCA procedures ensure the Senate will vote on passage of the House proposal.

Federal Student Aid Programs

The BCA also makes changes to the William D. Ford Federal Direct Loan (DL) program and the Federal Pell Grant program, two of the largest federal student aid programs authorized under Title IV of the Higher Education Act of 1965, as amended (HEA; P.L. 89-329).[7] The BCA amends the HEA by eliminating the availability of Subsidized Stafford Loans to graduate and professional students for periods of instruction beginning on or after July 1, 2012. The BCA also eliminates the authority of the Secretary of Education to offer one of the two types of repayment incentives on DL program loans first disbursed on or after July 1, 2012. CBO estimates these changes in the DL program would reduce direct spending by $9.6 billion over the FY2012-FY2016 period and $21.6 billion over the FY2012-FY2021 period.

Approximately $17 billion of the $21.6 billion in estimated savings from the changes in the DL program would be directed to the Pell Grant program for future general use. The BCA provides $10 billion in mandatory funding for FY2012, and $7 billion in mandatory funding for FY2013 for the program. These additional funds would reduce the amount of discretionary appropriations required in FY2012 and FY2013, although additional funding above the FY2011 discretionary level of approximately $23 billion may still be required in order to maintain the current eligibility parameters of the program in FY2012.

Expedited Procedures: General Observations

The BCA establishes legislative procedures for the expedited consideration of three legislative proposals: a resolution disapproving a debt increase, the joint committee bill, and a balanced budget constitutional amendment passed by the other chamber. The specifics of each of these procedures are contained in the relevant sections of this report, but the procedures are similar enough that it is possible to generalize about them.[8]

First and foremost, as is the case with all provisions of law that establish internal congressional procedures, either chamber can unilaterally decide to modify or otherwise disregard the procedures established by the BCA. Under the Constitution, each chamber may "determine the Rules of its Proceedings,"[9] and the BCA even explicitly acknowledges in two cases that the expedited procedures are being created with full acknowledgement of the right of either chamber to modify them.[10] To be clear, this is not to say that individual members or party leaders can deviate from the procedures established by the law without consequence; it is to say that the House or the Senate, acting under its regular rules, could modify the process without the permission of the other chamber. In the House, for example, this might be done by the approval of a special rule reported by the Committee on Rules. In the Senate, unanimous consent agreements might alter the specifics of the BCA's application.

Second, a motivation for the creation of expedited procedures is that they alter a fundamental feature of regular Senate procedure: the right of each Senator to engage in unlimited debate on a question. Under Senate rules, getting to a vote on most questions essentially requires either unanimous consent or the support of three-fifths of the Senate (normally 60 Senators). Even with the support of 60 Senators, considering legislation can be time consuming, since the cloture process used to limit consideration of any question takes several days and might have to be used in connection with more than one question. The procedures established for the consideration of the joint committee bill and for the consideration of the resolution disapproving a debt limit increase both allow the Senate to take up the legislation without debate, and therefore without the need for a multi-day, supermajority-vote cloture process. All of the expedited procedures created in the BCA place a time limit on floor consideration of the legislation, which means if the Senate has agreed to consider a measure, the Senate will have an opportunity to vote on it. All of the expedited procedures also prevent amendments.

In contrast to the Senate, in the House the same numerical majority that can pass a bill can set the terms for its consideration. For this reason, in part, the House majority might bring up the legislation as it normally does for other bills through adoption of a special rule, although this method is likely to preserve key elements of the expedited procedures including a prohibition on amendments, time restrictions on debate equally divided between a proponent and an opponent, and a prohibition on the motion to recommit.

Another motivation, however, for the creation of expedited procedures in both chambers is to establish a means of ensuring that the measure in question can be brought to the floor even if the leadership (and the committees of jurisdiction) do not seek its consideration. The statutory procedures established in the BCA provide a means by which a numerical majority, and not necessarily the partisan majority, can take up legislation in the House and Senate.

Debt Ceiling Increase and Disapproval Process

Increases in the Debt Limit in Three Installments

The Budget Control Act authorizes increases to the debt limit by at least \$2.1 trillion (and up to \$2.4 trillion), in three installments. First, upon the certification by the President that the debt subject to limit is within \$100 billion of the debt limit, the debt limit is increased by $400 billion immediately.[11] Second, if Congress does not enact into law a joint resolution of disapproval within 50 calendar days of receipt of the certification, the debt limit is increased by an additional $500 billion. If Congress enacts a joint resolution of disapproval (presumably over a presidential veto), the debt limit will not be increased and the Office of Management and Budget is required to sequester budgetary resources on a "pro rata" basis, subject to sequestration procedures and exemptions provided in Sections 253, 255, and 256 of the Balanced Budget and Emergency Deficit Control Act of 1985, as amended.[12]

Third, if the debt limit has been increased by the first $900 billion and upon another certification that the debt subject to limit is within $100 billion of the debt limit, Congress will have 15 calendar days of receipt of the certification to enact into law a joint resolution of disapproval to prevent another increase in the debt limit (again over a presumed presidential veto). If Congress does not enact such resolution, the debt limit is increased by one of three amounts: (1) $1.2 trillion; (2) an amount between $1.2 trillion and $1.5 trillion, if Congress passes and the President signs into law legislation introduced by the Joint Select Committee on Deficit Reduction;[13] or (3) $1.5 trillion, if a Constitutional amendment requiring a balanced budget is submitted to the states for ratification.

In summary, while an initial increase in the debt limit of $400 billion is effective immediately and not subject to congressional disapproval, subsequent additional increases of $500 billion and an amount between $1.2 trillion and $1.5 trillion are subject to congressional disapproval. That is, for either of the two subsequent additional increases in the debt limit, if Congress enacts a joint resolution of disapproval, the debt limit would not be increased by such amounts.

Expedited Procedures for Consideration of Disapproval Resolution

Introduction of a Qualifying Joint Resolution

A joint resolution disapproving either debt limit increase can be considered in both chambers under expedited procedures that limit debate and prevent amendment. A disapproval resolution would qualify for consideration under the expedited procedures of the BCA only if it meets specific content and timing criteria. The BCA mandates the exact language of a disapproval resolution: "That Congress disapproves of the President's exercise of authority to increase the debt limit, as exercised pursuant to the certification under section 3101A(a) of title 31, United States Code."[14] The BCA also provides the title for the joint resolution and states that it may not contain a preamble.

To qualify for expedited consideration, the joint resolution of disapproval also must be introduced by specific times. For the first opportunity to disapprove the increase in the debt limit, the resolution must be introduced on September 6, 7, 8, or 9, 2011.[15] For the opportunity to disapprove the second increase, the resolution must be introduced either the day the certification (that the debt subject to limit is within $100 billion of the debt limit) is received from the President or on any of the next three calendar days.

The BCA procedures apparently aim to ensure an opportunity for timely consideration of a disapproval resolution. In both chambers, any Member can introduce the joint resolution. Furthermore, if a chamber would otherwise not be in session when the President submits the second certification, the BCA requires the House Speaker and Senate majority leader (in consultation with the Senate minority leader) to reconvene their respective chambers within two calendar days after receiving the certification from the President.

The BCA anticipates introduction of a joint resolution of disapproval in both chambers.[16] Each chamber could initially consider its own joint resolution, although either eventually the House would need to pass the Senate joint resolution, or the Senate would need to pass the House joint resolution, in order to meet the constitutional requirement that the chambers pass precisely the same text in the same measure. The act also anticipates that each chamber will act on its own proposal by providing that if a chamber receives a joint resolution of disapproval from the other house before it has concluded consideration of its own resolution, it can consider or continue to consider its own legislation, but the final passage vote will be held on the resolution received from the other chamber.

Senate Consideration

After a Senator introduces the joint resolution, it will be placed directly on the Senate calendar instead of being referred to committee.[17] A motion to proceed to the consideration of the joint resolution will not be subject to debate if it is offered within a specified brief period after the certification is received from the President.[18] A non-debatable motion to proceed to a House-passed joint resolution of disapproval could also be made instead, as long as the Senate has not already considered a Senate resolution of disapproval. This non-debatable motion to proceed expedites the process of bringing a matter before the Senate.[19] Under the regular rules of the Senate, motions to proceed are usually subject to debate, so it therefore is sometimes necessary to gain the support of three-fifths of the Senate (60 Senators if no more than one vacancy) in order to end debate on the question of taking up a matter. In addition, if any motion to proceed to the disapproval resolution is disagreed to, another may be offered, although presumably only in the time frame provided. In addition, the BCA waives all points of order that could be raised against consideration of the joint resolution, and it also precludes several motions that could be used to delay its consideration.

If a majority of Senators voting agree to the motion to proceed, the joint resolution "shall remain the unfinished business until disposed of,"[20] meaning that it would require unanimous consent to turn to any other business and even the maturation of a cloture motion on another matter would not interrupt its consideration. The total time for consideration of the resolution is limited to 10 hours, equally divided between the majority and minority leader (or their designees). Because the time is controlled, Senators who wish to speak will need to be yielded time from one of the Leaders or another Senator acting as the floor manager. Because total *consideration* time is limited, time spent making requests or motions and time spent conducting quorum calls and votes, in addition to time spent in debate, will all count toward the 10 hour limit.[21] The Senate could consider the measure for less than 10 hours by unanimous consent, if Senators controlling time yield back time, or if a majority agree to a non-debatable motion to further limit debate. Several motions, most significantly any motion to amend the joint resolution, are precluded by the BCA, and appeals from decisions of the Chair are not debatable. A House-passed joint resolution of disapproval would be subject to the same procedures if no joint resolution is introduced or considered in the Senate.

Under the BCA, the Senate is to vote on passage of the joint resolution immediately after the expiration of the 10 hours of consideration, except that any Senator could request a live quorum call just prior to the vote.[22] If, at the time of the vote, the Senate has received the House version of the disapproval resolution, the final passage vote would occur on the House resolution instead of the Senate resolution.

House Consideration

In the House, after a joint resolution of disapproval is introduced, it is to be referred to committee as under the regular rules of the House. The BCA provides that if a committee fails to report within five calendar days after introduction, it will be automatically discharged and the joint resolution will be placed on the House calendar.

The BCA creates a special procedure for the House to take up the joint resolution, debate it for two hours, and take an up-or-down vote thereon without allowing Members to offer an amendment or a motion to recommit. The House could use these statutory procedures, or it might instead choose to take up the joint resolution through a special rule reported by the Rules Committee or by another method available under regular House rules.

Under the BCA procedures, once the committee has reported the measure (or been discharged), and no later than the sixth day after its introduction, any Member can move that the House take up the joint resolution. All points of order against the motion to proceed to the joint resolution are waived by the BCA, and the motion is not debatable; consequently the House would vote on the taking up the resolution immediately after the motion was made.[23]

If the House agrees to consider the joint resolution, it will be debated for up to two hours, equally divided and controlled by a proponent and an opponent. All points of order against the joint resolution are waived, and no amendments can be offered. Under ordinary House procedures the minority party is generally guaranteed a chance to offer a motion to recommit a bill prior to final passage, a motion that is effectively an opportunity to amend the bill.[24] No such opportunity is available under the statutory provisions.

If the House has received a joint resolution of disapproval from the Senate prior to voting on its own version of the joint resolution, the final passage vote in the House will occur on the Senate vehicle.

Procedures Following a Presidential Veto and the Enactment Deadline

Although only a majority of each chamber is necessary to agree to a resolution of disapproval, preventing an increase in the debt limit might ultimately require supermajority support. This is because if the Treasury has advised the President that further borrowing is required to meet existing commitments, the President might normally be expected to veto the congressional resolution of disapproval. Congress can override a presidential veto, but to do so would require the support of two-thirds of each chamber. The joint resolution of disapproval would be returned to the chamber that originated it, which under the statutory procedures will be the chamber that passes it first. Only if that chamber agreed to override the veto with a two-thirds vote would the second chamber also have an opportunity to vote on the question of overriding the veto.

The BCA limits debate on any veto message received in the Senate to one hour, equally divided between the majority and minority leaders or their designees.[25] Under regular Senate rules, the question of overriding the veto, and some other available motions that could displace consideration of the veto message, are subject to extended debate. The statutory debate limitation could allow a numerical majority of the Senate to get to a vote on the question of overriding the veto more quickly than might be possible under its regular rules. In the House, the veto message would be considered under its regular procedures which would normally limit debate to one hour.[26]

The BCA limits the time by which each potential disapproval resolution must be enacted into law. The disapproval resolution responding to the President's first certification has 50 calendar days from the time the Congress received the certification to be enacted into law. Similarly, a disapproval resolution in response to the President's second certification must be enacted into law within 15 calendar days from the time Congress receives the certification. As a result, successful enactment of a disapproval resolution might require not just passage by both chambers and presentment to the President but also, if the President returns the measure, a timely veto override vote in each chamber.

Under the Constitution, the President has up to 10 days, excluding Sundays, to either sign or veto a measure sent by the Congress.[27] If these days count toward the deadline for enactment, the length of time the President holds the measure could influence how much time, if any, Congress would have to act on a possible veto before the expiration of time allowed by the statute for enactment. Under the act, accordingly, if Congress passes a joint resolution of disapproval, the time that the President is in possession of the enrolled joint resolution is apparently not to be counted toward the 50 (or 15) days.[28]

STATUTORY LIMITS ON DISCRETIONARY SPENDING

Section 101 of the Budget Control Act of 2011 (BCA) amends Section 251 of the Balanced Budget and Emergency Deficit Control Act of 1985 (BBEDCA; Title II of P.L. 99-177, 2 U.S.C. 900-922) to establish 10-year adjustable statutory limits (or caps) on discretionary spending, enforced primarily through a sequestration process. Discretionary spending is provided and controlled through the annual appropriations process.[29] Statutory limits on discretionary spending were previously created by the Budget Enforcement Act of 1990 (Title XIII of P.L. 101-508), which also amended the BBEDCA, and twice were extended, in 1993 and 1997, but expired at the end of FY2002.[30] Section 104 of the BCA repeals the expiration date in the

BBEDCA, and thereby restores many features of the previous statutory discretionary limits, including the sequestration enforcement process.

The new statutory limits cap the amount of new budget authority for each fiscal year covering FY2012-FY2021 (see *Table 1*).[31] For FY2012 and FY2013, the spending limits are divided into two separate categories: security and nonsecurity. The security category includes discretionary spending for the Departments of Defense, Homeland Security, and Veterans Affairs, the National Nuclear Security Administration, the intelligence community management account, and all accounts in the international affairs budget function (budget function 150). The nonsecurity category includes discretionary spending in all other budget accounts. For FY2014-FY2021, the limits cap spending in a single category (specified as the discretionary category), which includes all discretionary spending in all budget accounts.

Adjustments

The BCA allows for the adjustment of the discretionary limits for six different purposes.[32] Five of the six adjustments effectively exempt certain discretionary spending from the statutory caps. The limits could be adjusted to accommodate: (1) changes in concepts and definitions; (2) appropriations designated as emergency requirements; (3) appropriations designated for Overseas Contingency Operations/Global War on Terrorism (such as for military activities in Iraq and Afghanistan); (4) appropriations for continuing disability reviews and redeterminations; (5) appropriations for controlling health care fraud and abuse; and (6) appropriations designated as being for disaster relief.

The first three adjustments are not capped, and therefore the statutory limits would be adjusted by the amounts meeting the conditions for the adjustment. Once a year, the Office of Management and Budget (OMB) can adjust the limits to reflect changes in concepts and definitions, in consultation with the Committees on Appropriations and Budget in each house. In addition, the limits must be adjusted by the amounts of appropriations designated as emergency requirements and those designated for Overseas Contingency Operations/Global War on Terrorism (OCO/GWOT) in statute and subsequently by the President.[33]

Table 1. Statutory Limits on Discretionary Spending and Certain Adjustments, FY2012-FY2021 (in billions of budget authority)

Fiscal Year	Discretionary Spending Limits[a]	Maximum Adjustments for Program Integrity Initiatives[b]
2012	$684 security	$0.893
	$359 nonsecurity	
2013	$686 security	$1.050
	$361 nonsecurity	
2014	$1,066	$1.253
2015	$1,086	$1.484
2016	$1,107	$1.561
2017	$1,131	$1.723
2018	$1,156	$1.743
2019	$1,182	$1.763
2020	$1,208	$1.784
2021	$1,234	$1.805

Source: Sections 251(b) (relating to adjustments) and 251(c) (relating to limits) of the Balanced Budget and Emergency Deficit Control Act of 1985, as amended by the Budget Control Act of 2011 (P.L. 112-25).

[a] The security category includes discretionary spending for the Departments of Defense, Homeland Security, and Veterans Affairs, the National Nuclear Security Administration, the intelligence community management account, and all accounts in the international affairs budget function (budget function 150). The nonsecurity category includes discretionary spending in all other budget accounts.

[b] The adjustments for program integrity initiatives include appropriations for "continuing disability reviews" under Disability Insurance and Supplemental Security Income (SSI) and "redeterminations" of eligibility under SSI beneficiaries and appropriations for the "health care fraud abuse program at the Department of Health and Human Services." Adjustments also are allowed to accommodate changes in concepts and definitions, as well as discretionary appropriations designated as emergency requirements, designated for Overseas Contingency Operations/Global War on Terrorism, and designated as being for disaster relief. The adjustments for the first three will equal the amounts so designated, with no limit on such adjustments, whereas the adjustments for the last one, disaster relief, is limited each year to an amount based on an historical average for such funding, as described in the text. OMB is required to calculate the initial such average within 30 days of enactment of the BCA.

The emergency and OCO/GWOT designations must be made on an account-by-account basis; this requirement presumably would preclude a blanket designation, for example, covering all appropriations provided in an appropriations act.

The three other adjustments are capped at certain amounts of appropriations for the specified purposes for each year. Two of the three adjustments allow for additional appropriations for program integrity initiatives—activities that are intended to produce a net reduction in federal spending;[34] the remaining adjustment allows for additional appropriations for relief activities associated with unexpected natural disasters. First, the adjustment for appropriations for "continuing disability reviews" under Disability Insurance and Supplemental Security Income (SSI) and "redeterminations" of eligibility under SSI beneficiaries would be the amount provided for such activities in excess of $273 million each year, with a maximum adjustment ranging from $623 million for FY2012 to $1,309 million for each of fiscal years 2017 through 2021, allowing for a total adjustment of $11,132 million over the entire period of FY2012-FY2021. Second, the adjustment for appropriations for the "health care fraud abuse program at the Department of Health and Human Services" would be the amount provided for such activities in excess of $311 million each year, with a maximum adjustment ranging from $270 million for FY2012 to $496 million for FY2021, allowing for a total adjustment of $3,927 million over the entire period of FY2012-FY2021. Finally, the adjustment for appropriations that Congress designates as being for disaster relief in statute may not exceed, in any year, "the average funding provided for disaster relief over the previous 10 years, excluding the highest and lowest years" plus the amount by which the appropriations so designated in the preceding fiscal year was less than the applicable average funding level.[35] For example, if in a fiscal year Congress designates $10 million less than the average level, then in the next fiscal year, the maximum adjustment could equal the applicable average level for that year plus the $10 million from the previous year.

Enforcement

The discretionary spending limits are primarily enforced through a sequestration process.[36] Sequestration is the largely across-the-board cancellation of budgetary resources (i.e., spending cuts) in nonexempt accounts.[37] If the final sequestration report (explained below), issued within 15 calendar days after the end of a session of Congress, indicates that discretionary appropriations within a category exceed the spending limit for that category, sequestration is triggered automatically. The President is required to issue a sequestration order canceling budgetary resources in nonexempt accounts, within the category in which the breach occurred, by an amount necessary to eliminate the breach.[38] For instance, if for FY2012 or FY2013 discretionary appropriations within the security category are enacted that results in a breach of the security category limit for either year, a sequestration of only security spending would occur to eliminate that breach. As noted above, for FY2014-FY2021, only one category exists for total discretionary appropriations; therefore, a sequestration, if necessary, would occur in that total discretionary appropriations category. Under the sequestration process, each nonexempt account is reduced by a uniform percentage, except that certain health and medical care accounts are limited to a 2% reduction, under Section 256(e) of the BBEDCA (as restored by Section 104 of the BCA).[39]

Along with the end-of-the-session sequester, a within-session sequester is required if an appropriation, such as a supplemental appropriation, causes a spending limit to be breached during a fiscal year. In this case, sequestration would occur 15 days after the enactment of the appropriation. If such a breach occurs in the last quarter of the fiscal year (i.e., July 1 through September 30), the applicable spending limit for the following fiscal year must be reduced by the amount of the breach.

The BCA also provides for the enforcement of the discretionary spending limits by points of order during the consideration of appropriations legislation in each house (new Section 314(e) of the Budget Act).[40] Because the caps limit the total amount of budget authority for the budget year, the order in which an individual appropriations bill is considered will affect whether or not it is subject to the point of order. The point of order most likely would apply to, and during the consideration of, the last appropriations act considered by each House, and any supplemental appropriations acts considered after the regular appropriations acts have been enacted.[41] In the Senate, a motion to waive the point of order requires an affirmative vote of three-fifths of Senators, duly chosen and sworn (i.e., 60 Senators if there is no more than one vacancy);[42] in the House, a special rule waiving the point of order would require an affirmative majority vote.

Reports

OMB and CBO are required to issue several reports throughout each year to assist Congress in complying with the spending limits and, in the case of OMB's final sequestration report, to trigger the sequestration of budgetary resources, if any limit is exceeded.[43] First, for each appropriations act signed into law, OMB is required to issue a cost estimate of the legislation within seven days of its enactment; CBO is required to provide to OMB its cost estimate of such legislation as soon as practicable after Congress completes action on such legislation. Second, three separate sequestration reports are required, at certain times during the year, to provide the status of the discretionary spending limits, including any appropriate adjustments to the limits: (1) a sequestration preview report, (2) a sequestration update report, and (3) a final sequestration report.[44] OMB is required to issue such reports with the President's budget submission, by August 20, and 15 days after the end of a session, respectively; CBO is required to issue its own sequestration update and final sequestration reports five days prior to OMB's reports.[45] Most importantly, OMB's final sequestration report generally is the only report triggering a sequester. Therefore, if a breach has occurred, the final report must include the percentage reduction and amount of budgetary resources to be sequestered, for each affected budget account.

Rules Related to Provisions Designated as Emergency in the House

Section 105(a)(3) of the BCA amends the Congressional Budget Act to establish certain procedural rules relating to the treatment of, and consideration of legislation containing, provisions designated as an emergency requirement.[46] In general, the rules allow the House to exempt from congressional budget constraints provisions designated as emergency requirements pursuant to the BBEDCA, as amended by the BCA. They also provide opportunities for Members to strike such designations and offer proposals to offset the budgetary effects of a designated provision.

First, any new discretionary appropriations designated as an emergency requirement pursuant to Section 251(b)(2)(A) of the BBEDCA will not be counted for purposes of Titles III and IV of the Budget Act.[47] As explained above (see "Adjustments" section), under Section 251(b)(2)(A) of the BBEDCA, the statutory discretionary spending limits may be adjusted to accommodate appropriations designated, on an account-by-account basis, as emergency requirements.[48] The rules change effectively allows the House to exempt such spending from certain spending constraints, such as the appropriations subcommittee allocations under Section 302(b) of the Budget Act.

Second, new Section 314(d)(2)(B) of the Budget Act provides that the budgetary effects of a motion to strike a designation (presumably an emergency designation)[49] shall not be counted for purposes of Titles III and IV of the Budget Act and the House Standing Rules. The rule would allow a Member to offer an amendment to strike the designation without being subject to a point of order. Without this rule, a motion to strike an emergency designation contained in an appropriations act, for example, would likely be subject to a point of order under Section 302(f) of the Budget Act because striking the designation would cause the applicable new budget authority to be counted and therefore likely cause the appropriations bill to exceed its Section 302(b) allocation.[50]

Finally, new Section 314(d)(2)(C) of the Budget Act provides that an amendment proposing to strike an emergency designation and also to reduce "each amount appropriated or otherwise made available" shall be in order at any time during the reading of a bill for amendment. The purpose of such an amendment would presumably be to make across-the-board reductions in spending already subject to the applicable spending cap sufficient to accommodate the appropriation newly being subjected to the spending constraint. Without this rule, such an amendment, making across-the-board reductions throughout the bill, generally would not be in order for at least three reasons: (1) it proposes to amend a paragraph or section in a bill not yet read for amendment; (2) it proposes to amend a paragraph or section already read for amendment; and (3) it proposes to amend the bill in more than one place.[51] Under the rule, nevertheless, such an amendment presumably would be subject to a demand for a division of the question (thereby forcing separate votes on striking the designation and reducing the appropriated amounts).

SENATE BUDGET ENFORCEMENT FOR FY2012 AND FY2013

Section 106 of the Budget Control Act establishes certain procedural provisions for the purpose of budget enforcement for FY2012 and FY2013 that apply in the Senate only, which expire, with respect to each of these fiscal years, if Congress adopts a budget resolution for that year. The provisions would establish budget levels enforceable in the Senate, including constraints on spending provided in appropriations acts for FY2012 and FY2013, if the House and Senate are not able to agree on a budget resolution for the respective fiscal year.[52]

Specifically, these procedural provisions of the BCA require the chair of the Senate Budget Committee (SBC) to file a statement of levels of various budgetary amounts that would ordinarily be established by the budget resolution for FY2012, including committee spending allocations, aggregate spending and revenue levels, and Social Security revenue and outlay levels, covering the period FY2011-FY2021.[53] The budget levels filed must be consistent with the statutory discretionary spending limits, established by Section 101 of the BCA, and with CBO's March 2011 baseline levels (adjusted to account for the budgetary effects of the BCA, as well as of any other legislation enacted prior to the BCA).[54] Under the provisions of Section 106 of the BCA, these levels are to have the same force and effect as if they were included and associated with a budget resolution for FY2012 adopted by Congress.

The SBC chair would also be required to file such budget levels covering the period FY2012- FY2022, by April 15, 2012, consistent with the same baseline parameters, and such levels would have the same force and effect as if they were included and associated with a budget resolution for FY2013 adopted by Congress.

Finally, the SBC chair is required to reduce the balances on the Senate Pay-As-You-Go (PAYGO) ledger to zero. The Senate PAYGO rule generally requires that any legislation projected to increase direct spending or reduce revenues must also include equivalent amounts of direct spending cuts, revenue increases, or a combination of the two, so that the legislation does not increase the on-budget deficit over a six-year period and an 11-year period.[55] The PAYGO ledger records any projected deficit reduction resulting from legislation (except reconciliation legislation) enacted since the beginning of the calendar year and not accounted for in the baseline, as defined by the rule.

Therefore, reducing the balance to zero would prevent such balances (in particular, those resulting from the deficit reduction included in the BCA) from being used to offset increases in the deficit resulting from legislation subsequently considered in the Senate.

JOINT SELECT COMMITTEE ON DEFICIT REDUCTION

Title IV of the Budget Control Act establishes a Joint Select Committee on Deficit Reduction, composed of an equal number of Senators and Members of the House, and instructs it to develop a proposal that would reduce the deficit by at least $1.5 trillion over FY2012 to FY2021. The BCA provides no other guidelines regarding the policy content of the proposal. The proposal, if reported by a majority of the joint committee by November 23, 2011, could be considered by each chamber under special procedures that prevent amendment and limit debate. The expedited procedures represent a significant divergence from regular Senate procedures, under which it can generally become necessary to obtain agreement among at least three-fifths of the Senate (normally 60 Senators) in order to bring debate to a close and the chamber to a vote on a matter. The expedited procedures in each chamber will only apply to a joint committee bill passed on or before December 23, 2011. If a joint committee bill reducing the deficit by at least $1.2 trillion is not signed into law by January 15, 2012, then the process of automatic spending reduction created by the BCA will begin to occur in January of 2013.

The BCA identifies several other specific actions the joint committee and Congress are expected to take by certain dates (*Appendix B, Table B-1*). In some cases, the BCA establishes direct, procedural consequences if an action is not completed by a stated time. In other cases, there is no immediate procedural result if an action is not taken, or if it is not taken by a stated deadline. Ultimately, if the joint committee bill does not become law, then the consequence is the automatic spending reduction process explained in the following section of this report.

Establishment of the Joint Committee

Membership

Party leaders appointed the 12 members of the Joint Select Committee on Deficit Reduction by the target date established in the BCA of August 16,

2011. [56] The Speaker of the House, the House minority leader, the Senate majority leader, and the Senate minority leader each appointed three members. From among these 12 joint committee members, the Senate majority leader appointed a co-chair and the House Speaker appointed the other co-chair. If any seat on the joint committee becomes vacant, due to resignation or otherwise, the leader who appointed the member vacating the seat would appoint a replacement within 14 days. Members of the joint committee will serve until its termination on January 31, 2012. Committee members must comply with the ethics rules of the their respective chambers (Section 401(c)(2)).[57]

Staffing and Funding[58]

The co-chairs jointly are to hire a staff director as well as other staff for the committee. The co-chairs are also empowered to fix the compensation of staff "within guidelines for employees of the Senate and following all applicable rules and employment requirements of the Senate."[59] Staff of the committee must comply with ethics rules of the Senate.[60] The BCA directs federal agencies to "provide technical assistance" if requested in writing by the co-chairs.[61]

Funding for the committee is provided equally from House and Senate appropriations accounts. The committee is "authorized to incur expenses in the same manner and under the same conditions as the Joint Economic Committee."[62]

Development of the Joint Committee Recommendations

The Budget Control Act requires the joint committee to hold its first meeting no later than September 16, 2011. The committees of the House and Senate may submit recommendations regarding deficit reduction to the joint committee, for which the BCA establishes a deadline of October 14, 2011. The act neither requires committees to submit recommendations nor requires the joint committee to consider the recommendations. Generally, however, both chambers rely on the expertise of committees with jurisdiction over policy matters, and ultimately, of course, the joint committee proposal can succeed only with the support of a numerical majority in both chambers.

The joint committee is expected to develop a report of its findings and recommendations as well as legislative language to carry out the recommendations. The report is required to contain a cost estimate prepared by

CBO, and the legislation is required to include a "statement of the deficit reduction achieved by the legislation over the period of fiscal years 2012 to 2021."[63] The report may contain supplemental, additional or minority views, provided that a joint committee member gave notice of the intent to submit such views at the time of the vote on the report and submitted the views in writing to the committee staff director within 3 calendar days of the vote. The BCA places no other requirements on the content of the report or on the legislative language.[64] It could recommend changes to revenue, spending, or both; it might even propose new budget enforcement mechanisms.

The joint committee must vote on proposed legislative language as well as an accompanying report by November 23, 2011. If the committee does not vote by that date, no legislation will be eligible for consideration under the expedited procedures of the BCA. Support from a majority of the joint committee, or seven members if no vacancies, is necessary to approve the report and the legislative language. If the language and report are approved, both must be transmitted to the President, Vice President, Speaker of the House, and majority and minority leaders of both chambers by December 2, 2011.

Procedures for the Operation of Joint Committee Meetings

Title IV of the Budget Control Act also establishes several rules concerning the operation of joint committee meetings and hearings. Some of these rules resemble the existing standing rules of each chamber; others are unique to the joint committee.

The BCA states that a quorum of the joint committee, or the number of members required to be present for the conduct of business, is seven. This is the minimum number of members who must be present at any vote or any meeting of the committee, including hearings. If seven members are not present, then presumably any member of the committee could make a point of order, under the BCA, that a quorum is not present. If the member presiding determined that a quorum was not present, and the joint committee could not establish a quorum, the committee presumably would adjourn. Most committees of the House and Senate have lower quorum requirements, often just two members, for the receipt of testimony, and often one-third for business meetings other than the vote to report. The BCA also precludes "proxy voting," or the practice, common in the Senate but forbidden by House rules, of allowing another member of a committee (usually the chair or ranking member) to cast a vote for a member who is not present. Furthermore, the agenda for any meeting must be made available to all members of the joint committee at least 48 hours ahead of time.

The BCA grants the joint committee the authority to conduct hearings, including the power to require witness attendance and submission of documentation. The authority is similar to that granted to House committees in House Rule XI clause 2(m)(1) and to Senate committees in Senate Rule XXVI, paragraph 1. The statements of any witnesses appearing before the joint committee must be submitted in writing two calendar days prior to the hearing, unless the co-chairs waive the requirement. Many standing committees rules in both chambers require witness testimony to be submitted two days in advance, longer than the one day required by the Senate (Rule XXVI, paragraph 4(b)) and more specific than the House rule (House Rule XI, clause 2(g)(4) which states that committees shall require written statements in advance). Finally, the co-chairs must publicly announce any hearings seven days in advance, unless they determine there is good cause to provide less notice. The hearing notice requirement is similar to the week required under House and Senate rules (House Rule XI, clause 2 (g)(3) and Senate Rule XXVI, paragraph 4).

The joint committee cannot vote on the question of approving the report or legislative language unless CBO cost estimates mentioned above have been available to its members for at least 48 hours. After any such vote, the report, legislative language, and record of the vote must "promptly"[65] be made available to the public.

All other regulations concerning the internal operations of the committee will be established by the joint committee itself. Under House rules, the joint committee is required to adopt written rules of procedure.[66] It is not clear what effect a House-only rule could have on a bicameral entity, but, if the House rule is followed, the joint committee will meet in public to consider its rules (unless a majority agree by recorded vote to close the meeting).[67]

Expedited Procedures for Consideration of the Joint Committee Bill

Introduction and Referral of Joint Committee Bill in Both Chambers

If the joint committee transmits its report and proposed legislative language, the Budget Control Act requires the House majority leader (or his designee) and the Senate majority leader (or his designee) to each introduce the proposed language, without change, as a bill. The leaders (or designees) will introduce the legislation "by request," which signals that the act of introduction is not necessarily a personal endorsement of the bill. Two bills will therefore be introduced in Congress, with identical text, but with different numbers (one will be an S. numbered bill and the other an H.R. numbered bill). The House and Senate can then each initially consider its own bill.[68] To meet the Constitutional requirement that both chambers agree to the same legislative measure with the same text, the act provides a means (described in more detail below) for one chamber to vote on final passage of the bill received from the other chamber instead of its own bill. The Constitution also requires that bills affecting revenues originate in the House, and for that reason Section 402(e)(2) ensures that if the joint committee bill contains revenue provisions, it will be the House bill that is eventually presented to the President.

In the Senate, the majority leader or his designee is to introduce the legislative language as the joint committee bill on the first calendar day that the Senate is in session after the joint committee proposal is submitted. The BCA provides for joint referral of the legislation to all committees of jurisdiction. This procedure contrasts with regular Senate practice, under which legislation is, with few exceptions, referred to just one committee, the one with jurisdiction over the subject matter predominant in the bill (Senate Rule XVII, paragraph 1), or, if the bill contains any revenue provisions, typically just to the Committee on Finance. Any committee to which the bill is referred is required to report it without amendment by December 9, 2011; any committee that fails to report by that time will be automatically discharged and the bill will be placed on the Senate legislative calendar, where it is available to be taken up by the full chamber. In this way, the BCA appears to mandate referral while also preventing any committee from blocking floor consideration.[69]

In the House, the majority leader or his designee is to introduce the proposed language as the joint committee bill on the first legislative day[70] after the joint committee proposal is transmitted. The bill will be referred under regular House rules by the Speaker to every committee having jurisdiction over a provision of the bill. Each such committee can report the legislation—favorably, unfavorably, or without recommendation—but cannot report it with amendment and are required to report by December 9, 2011. The BCA creates a privileged motion by which the House could discharge any committee that does not report by the deadline, although general rules also provide the House majority with other means to bring the bill to the floor.

Senate Floor Action

The Senate could consider a bill introduced pursuant to the Budget Control Act under special procedures that differ considerably from general Senate rules. Decision-making in the Senate is shaped by the ability of individual Senators to "filibuster," or to take actions to prevent (or delay) a matter from coming to a vote. To get to a vote on a question in the Senate can require either the consent of every single Senator, or the cloture process, which itself can be time-consuming. A cloture motion is not voted on until two days of session after it is filed. If cloture is successfully invoked by a vote of three-fifths of Senators duly chosen and sworn (60 Senators if there is no more than one vacancy), then consideration of the question can continue for up to 30 additional hours. The time required for the cloture process can be compounded since getting to a final passage vote on a bill might require a successful cloture process on several questions: for example, on the question of taking up the bill, on a major amendment to the bill, and on the bill itself.[71]

The special procedures established in the Budget Control Act are discussed in detail below, but in general they can be understood to expedite the Senate floor process by providing that the bill be taken up without debate and by imposing a time limit on consideration of the bill, thereby avoiding the need to invoke cloture on any question.

Privileged for Consideration

Under the Budget Control Act, a joint committee bill could be promptly brought before the Senate. Once a qualifying bill is on the Senate calendar, the majority leader (or his designee) can move to proceed to the bill. After the bill has been on the calendar for two days of session, any Senator can move that the Senate proceed to the bill. In either case, the motion to proceed to the bill is not debatable and a simple majority vote is all that is needed to take up the bill. If past practice on taking up other measures privileged for consideration is any guide, the Senate might reach a consensus to begin consideration of the bill and not conduct a roll call vote on the motion to proceed.[72] The BCA further allows multiple opportunities for proponents to propose that the bill be taken up; even if the Senate disagrees to one motion to proceed to the joint committee bill, additional such motions could be offered and would not be subject to debate.

This BCA procedure differs from regular Senate rules, under which most motions to proceed are debatable. The ability to take up a matter without debate is potentially significant in the Senate. If there is opposition to calling up a bill, the Senate might need to go through the cloture process, as described above, even to reach a vote on the motion to proceed to the bill.

The Budget Control Act addresses additional motions and actions to help ensure that the Senate decide on the question of taking up the bill without delay. It precludes motions to postpone as well as motions to reconsider the vote, motions that if allowed could potentially lead to additional time-consuming roll call votes. It also prevents any Senator from making a point of order against consideration of the joint committee bill. In addition, the bill is apparently given special standing in relation to pending matters on which cloture has already been invoked. Under the BCA, the motion to proceed is in order "Notwithstanding Rule XXII" (the cloture rule), suggesting that perhaps even if the Senate is considering a matter on which cloture has been invoked, which would ordinarily require consideration until disposed of, the motion to proceed to the joint committee bill would be in order.

Privileged for Disposition

If the motion to proceed to the joint committee bill is agreed to, then under the BCA it "shall remain the unfinished business until disposed of."[73] This means that, absent unanimous consent, the Senate cannot turn to other legislative or executive business. A motion to proceed to another bill or to enter executive session to consider a nomination, for example, would not be in order. Nor would consideration of the joint committee bill be interrupted by the maturation of a cloture motion filed on a different pending matter two days of session before the joint committee bill was taken up. The bill itself is also protected from any points of order.

Under the BCA, no amendments can be proposed to the joint committee bill. Senators can debate the bill, but they cannot propose changes to it. This is a departure from regular Senate procedure, under which Senators can offer amendments and, in fact, can offer them on any topic under most circumstances. Consideration of the bill under the BCA is limited to a maximum of 30 hours.[74]

All the time spent on consideration of the bill, including time spent debating related motions, voting, and in quorum calls, would count against the 30 hours. In this respect, the expedited procedure would operate similarly to the 30-hour time cap on consideration after cloture is invoked on a bill.[75]

The Budget Control Act, however, also provides that the 30 hours be controlled by the party leaders, which is different from proceedings under cloture. Under controlled time, Senators are yielded blocks of time for debate from party leaders or bill managers (or their designees). Thus, for consideration of the joint committee bill, each party leader would be granted 15 hours, and the party leader would then decide who could speak, for how long, and in what order.[76] Similar terms apply, under the Congressional Budget Act of 1974, during consideration of a budget resolution or a reconciliation bill in the Senate. Frequently, time is also controlled in the Senate by unanimous consent agreements. Under the regular rules of the Senate, however, time is not controlled, there is no limit placed on how long a Senator can speak, and Senators speak in the order they seek recognition from the presiding officer.

In an apparent effort to streamline Senate procedures, the BCA includes several other provisions restricting the motions that can normally be made or the length they could otherwise be debated. Under the BCA, in addition to the prohibition on amendments, it is not in order to offer a motion to postpone or a motion to recommit the bill. Appeals from decisions of the chair relating to Senate rules are not debatable under the act. Any other motions that might be offered or appeals that might be made are debatable for just one hour each (included under the total cap of 30 hours) equally divided between those favoring and opposing the motion.

When the time for consideration of the joint committee bill has expired, then under the BCA the Senate is to vote on passage of the bill. Just as under regular Senate rules, passing the bill would require support from a simple majority of Senators voting, or 51 if all Senators vote and there are no vacancies. At the request of any Senator, there could be a live quorum call prior to the final passage vote. The purpose of allowing a quorum call presumably is to provide an opportunity to bring Senators to the floor for the vote, if necessary. The vote on passage is to occur no later than December 23, 2011; after that time, the special procedures for consideration of the bill will not longer apply.[77]

House Floor Action

Under the Terms of the Budget Control Act

The BCA creates special procedures that ensure that the House could bring the Joint committee bill to the floor even if the committees of jurisdiction and party leadership do not seek its consideration. If a committee does not report by December 9, 2011, a Member could make a privileged motion to discharge the committee from consideration. The motion is debatable for 20 minutes, and if it is agreed to the measure would be immediately pending before the House. Furthermore, if the committee or committees do report,[78] any Member could make a non-debatable motion that the House proceed to consider the joint committee bill.

Once the House has agreed to bring the bill to the floor, the BCA procedures provide that the House is to consider the legislation for two hours without an opportunity for amendment and then vote on final passage. All points of order against the bill and against its consideration are considered waived. Under ordinary House procedures the minority party is generally guaranteed a chance to offer a motion to recommit the bill before final passage,[79] but no such opportunity is available under the statutory procedures. One motion is in order to limit debate time further.

The BCA provides a procedure for any numerical majority to take up and pass a bill without delay, but it also precludes individual members or minority factions from slowing down the business of the House by offering repetitive motions. For example, once one motion to discharge a committee is disposed of (perhaps by a motion to table—or kill—the discharge proposal) another such motion is not in order. Similarly, if the House disposes of a motion to proceed to the joint committee bill, perhaps because a numerical majority decline to take it up, further motions to proceed to the joint committee bill are not in order. No motions to reconsider votes are permitted.

The House, like the Senate, is required under the BCA to pass the bill by December 23, 2011. If the bill is not passed by both chambers at the end of that day, then it cannot be considered under the expedited procedures of the BCA.[80]

Option to Consider the Bill under the Terms of a Special Rule

The House has the option, however, of considering the joint committee bill under a special rule reported by the Rules Committee in the same way that other major legislation is brought before the House for consideration.[81] When the House considers measures eligible for expedited procedures under other statutes, such as the Congressional Budget Act of 1974 and the Trade Act of 1974, it typically does so not under the statutory expedited procedures but under a special rule.

The House might choose this form of consideration in order to customize the terms of consideration (debate time could differ, for example, from the two hours provided under the BCA). It also might choose to bring the measure up by special rule in order to avoid procedural steps created by the BCA that are uncommon in current House practice. In fact, one reason to use a special rule might be because it is a manner of proceeding with which all Members of the House are familiar.

Even if the House does bring up the joint committee bill by rule, it is unlikely that amendments to the bill will be made in order unless there is reason to expect the Senate could expeditiously consider the measure under its regular rules. If the House were to amend the bill, the bill would be ineligible for expedited consideration in the Senate. The House-amended text would be different from that recommended by the Joint committee, and thus it would no longer meet the definition of a joint committee bill under the BCA. [82] If prior practice under statutory expedited procedures is a guide, it is also unlikely that a motion to recommit would be made in order if the bill were brought up by special rule.[83] Since the motion to recommit with instructions is effectively an opportunity to amend a bill, a successful motion to recommit with instructions would make the bill ineligible for expedited consideration in the Senate.

Passage Vote and Subsequent Action

Because the joint committee bills introduced in each chamber are both required to consist of the legislative text proposed by the joint committee, and because no amendments are in order in either chamber, if each chamber passes its bill, both measures will be identical. No conference committee or other means of resolving policy differences between the chambers will be necessary. Under the Constitution, however, it is necessary for both chambers to pass the same measure. In other words, even if each chamber passes its own numbered bill (for example, the House passes H.R. 2345 and the Senate passes S. 6789), and the texts of those two bills are identical, either the House must pass the Senate bill or the Senate must pass the House bill. Under the Budget Control Act, Congress will meet this requirement by providing that the joint committee bill that passes a chamber first will be the bill that is sent to the President.

More specifically, it provides that if the Senate receives the House joint committee bill before it has passed its own joint committee bill, the Senate will consider its own bill up until the point of final passage. When it is time to vote on final passage, the vote will occur on the identical House bill. If the Senate passes its bill before it receives the House companion measure, then it will send its bill to the House, and the House will vote on the Senate bill. If the joint committee bill has any provisions affecting revenue, however, then the Senate will vote on the identical House bill when received, regardless of which chamber has passed its bill first.

If the President vetoes the joint committee bill, each chamber could override the President's veto with a two-thirds vote.[84] The BCA limits debate on any veto message received in the Senate to one hour, equally divided between the majority and minority leaders or their designees. Under regular

Senate rules, the question of overriding the veto, and some other available motions that could displace consideration of the veto message, are subject to extended debate. The statutory debate limitation could allow the Senate to more quickly get to a vote on the question of overriding the veto than might be possible under the regular rules. In the House, the veto message would be considered under its regular procedures normally permitting one hour of debate. The deadline for enactment—passage by both chambers and signature by the President—to prevent an automatic spending reduction process is January 15, 2012.

BUDGET GOAL ENFORCEMENT: SPENDING REDUCTION TRIGGER

Section 302 of the Budget Control Act of 2011 establishes an automatic process to reduce spending, beginning in 2013, unless a joint committee bill reducing the deficit by at least $1.2 trillion over the period covering FY2012-FY2021 is enacted by January 15, 2012.[85] The process presumably is intended to encourage agreement on such deficit reduction, either by enacting the joint committee proposal by the deadline at the end of 2011, or possibly by enacting other legislation (through existing congressional procedures) by the beginning of 2013, when the automatic process would begin to make reductions. In effect, if Congress and the President do not act to reduce the deficit by $1.2 billion through the enactment of legislation, then spending reductions are automatically made, unless Congress and the President agree by statute to repeal or modify the automatic process.

The spending reduction process is triggered automatically if legislation introduced by the joint committee is not enacted, or if it is enacted, but it does not reduce the deficit by at least $1.2 trillion over the period covering FY2012-FY2021. Therefore, if a joint committee bill is enacted, but it reduces the deficit by only $900 billion, for example, the automatic process would still be triggered to make up the remainder.

If triggered, the automatic spending reduction process entails four key steps:

- the statutory discretionary spending limits for FY2013-FY2021 are revised, by redefining the security and nonsecurity categories and by extending such categories through FY2021;

- the amount of spending reduction required for each year is calculated and divided equally between two categories—defense and nondefense;
- the annual amount of spending reductions required each year in each of these categories is further divided proportionally between discretionary appropriations and direct spending programs (excluding certain programs and activities) within each category; and
- the spending reductions required in each year (FY2013-FY2021) are achieved through a combination of sequestration and the downward adjustment of the revised discretionary spending limits.

Each of these steps is described in detail below, to explain how the spending reductions would be achieved in the event the automatic process is triggered.

Revising Statutory Limits on Discretionary Spending

First, the statutory discretionary spending limits for FY2013-FY2021, established under Section 101 of the BCA, are revised: (1) to redefine the security and nonsecurity categories; and (2) to set annual limits for each of these categories through FY2021.[86] The revised categories basically divide the original discretionary spending limits between defense and nondefense accounts; at this point, the total amount of discretionary spending allowed under the limits is not yet reduced (see Table 2). In contrast to the original discretionary limits under Section 251 of the BBEDCA, as amended by the BCA, the security category is revised to include discretionary appropriations classified as budget function 050 (national defense) only.[87] The nonsecurity category is revised to include all other discretionary appropriations; the other discretionary appropriations not in budget function 050 ("National Defense") included in the original security category are essentially transferred to the revised nonsecurity category. By setting annual limits for the revised categories through FY2021, the revised limits extend the "firewall" between different spending categories beyond the original two-year firewalls (for FY2012 and FY2013). Both changes to the discretionary spending limits presumably facilitate the equal split of the required spending reduction between defense and nondefense accounts over the nine years through FY2021, as required in the next steps.

Table 2. Revised Statutory Limits on Discretionary Spending if Automatic Spending Reduction Process is Triggered (in billions of budget authority)

		Revised Limits	
Fiscal Year	Original Limits	Revised Security Category	Revised Nonsecurity Category
2013	$1,047[a]	$546	$501
2014	$1,066	$556	$510
2015	$1,086	$566	$520
2016	$1,107	$577	$530
2017	$1,131	$590	$541
2018	$1,156	$603	$553
2019	$1,182	$616	$566
2020	$1,208	$630	$578
2021	$1,234	$644	$590

Source: Sections 251(c) (relating to original limits) and 251A(2) (relating to revised limits) of the Balanced Budget and Emergency Deficit Control Act of 1985, as amended by the Budget Control Act of 2011 (P.L. 112- 25).

Notes: The revised security category includes discretionary appropriations classified as budget function 050 ("National Defense") only; the revised nonsecurity category includes all other discretionary appropriations. Under the automatic spending reduction process, revised limits for FY2014-FY2021 are subsequently adjusted downward each year by an amount based on the calculation specified in the BCA. The revised limits for FY2013 are not adjusted downward; instead, discretionary appropriations for FY2013 are sequestered (i.e., cut) by the calculated amounts. After the sequestration, it appears that subsequent discretionary appropriations for FY2013 presumably could be provided, as long as the total within a category for the year did not exceed a revised limit.

[a] For FY2013, the original spending limits are divided into the two separate categories of security ($686 billion) and nonsecurity ($361 billion); for definitions of original security and nonsecurity categories, see "Statutory Limits on Discretionary Spending" section, above.

Calculating the Spending Reductions

Second, OMB is required to calculate the amount of deficit reduction required to be achieved in the defense and nondefense budget functions each year through this automatic process. The calculation involves five steps: (1) begin with $1.2 trillion (the budget goal); (2) subtract the amount of deficit reduction in the joint committee bill, if enacted;[88] (3) subtract 18% of thedifference, attributable to debt service; (4) divide by nine, to allocate the spending reductions equally across the nine FY2013-FY2021; and (5) divide by two, to allocate the spending reductions between defense and nondefense functions. Again, this calculation provides the amount of spending reductions required from each of the two categories of defense and nondefense for each fiscal year covering FY2013-FY2021.

Table 3 provides two hypothetical illustrations of the calculations to be required, if the automatic process is triggered. In the first illustration, for example, $900 billion of deficit reduction is achieved through the enactment of a joint committee bill. In this case, the automatic process would require $13.7 billion each in spending reductions within the defense function and within the total of all other budget functions (nondefense functions) each year.

Table 3. Hypothetical Calculations of Reductions Required in Defense and Nondefense Spending if Automatic Spending Reduction Process is Triggered

Description of Calculation	Hypothetical Illustration #1: Enactment of Joint Committee Bill Reducing Deficit by $900 Billion	Hypothetical Illustration #2: Joint Committee Bill Is Not Enacted (i.e., No Deficit Reduction)
Budget goal	$1,200 billion	$1,200 billion
Subtract amount of deficit reduction in joint committee bill, if enacted	$1,200 billion-$900 billion = $300 billion	$1,200 billion-$0 billion = $1,200 billion
Multiply difference by 18%, to determine amount attributable to debt service	$300 billion * 0.18 = $54 billion	$1,200 billion * 0.18 = $216 billion
Subtract the 18%, to account for debt service savings	$300 billion - $54 billion = $246 billion	$1,200 billion-$216 billion = $984 billion
Divide by 9, to determine spending cuts for each year, FY2013-FY2021	$246 billion / 9 = $27.3 billion	$984 billion / 9 = $109.3 billion
Divide by 2, to allocate between defense and nondefense spending	$27.3 billion / 2 = $13.7 billion	$109.3 billion / 2 = $54.7 billion

Source: Formula provided in Section 251A(3) of the Balanced Budget and Emergency Deficit Control Act of 1985, as amended by the Budget Control Act of 2011 (P.L. 112-25). Amounts of deficit reduction resulting from joint Committee bill are hypothetical.

The third step is that the annual amount of spending reductions required in each of these categories is further divided proportionally between discretionary and nonexempt direct spending within each category.[89] These calculations, as set forth in the Budget Control Act, yield four amounts of required spending reductions, respectively in (1) defense discretionary appropriations, (2) defense direct spending, (3) nondefense discretionary appropriations, and (4) nondefense direct spending.[90]

Implementing the Required Spending Reductions

Finally, the required spending reductions are achieved each year (FY2013-FY2021) through a combination of a sequestration process[91] and the downward adjustment of the *revised discretionary spending limits.* Specifically, the reductions required are implemented in three parts: (1) for discretionary spending for FY2013, a sequestration of budgetary resources in that year; (2) for discretionary spending for FY2014-FY2021, a downward adjustment of the *revised discretionary spending limits*; and (3) for direct spending, a sequestration of budgetary resources in each year from FY2013 through FY2021.

In general, the sequestration process involves the cancellation of budgetary resources (i.e., spending cuts) in nonexempt programs and accounts.[92] Certain programs and activities are exempt from any sequestration.[93] Such programs include Social Security, Medicaid, and federal retirement and disability programs, among many others, as provided by Section 255 of the BBEDCA (as restored by Section 104 of the BCA).[94] In addition, the sequestration process is governed by general and special rules, as provided in the BCA, Section 6 of the Statutory Pay-As-You-Go Act of 2010 (Title I of P.L. 111-139), and Section 256 of the BBEDCA, including a 2% limit on any reductions in spending for Medicare and for certain health care programs.

The BCA requires OMB to calculate, in the manner specified above, and the President to order a sequestration of nonexempt discretionary appropriations for FY2013, and of nonexempt direct spending for FY2013 and for each year through FY2021. The sequestration for FY2013 is to occur on January 2, 2013, and the sequestrations for subsequent years are to occur on the date the sequestration preview report is issued (i.e., with the President's budget submission).[95] Generally, under the sequestration process, each nonexempt account is reduced by a uniform percentage necessary to achieve the reductions required.[96] For example, if for FY2013 hypothetically \$54.2 billion in spending reductions are required in defense discretionary appropriations, and assuming the total amount of nonexempt defense discretionary appropriations is \$546 billion, then each nonexempt account within the defense function would be reduced by 9.9%. Within the nondefense category, the BCA requires that OMB increase the reductions required in discretionary appropriations and nonexempt non-Medicare spending by a uniform percentage to in effect offset the reductions not achieved in Medicare spending as a result of the 2% limit.

Finally, on the date the sequestration preview report is issued (i.e., with the President's budget submission), for each year covering FY2014-FY2021, OMB is required to adjust downward the *revised statutory limits on discretionary spending* for each category by the amount of spending reduction required within each category for that year, calculated in the manner described above. As a result, the spending reductions in discretionary appropriations for FY2014-FY2021 are achieved by further limiting the maximum amount that may be appropriated in each category for each year. In contrast to the spending reductions achieved through sequestration for FY2013, the lower limits for subsequent fiscal years will provide Congress and the President the opportunity to determine the manner in which the reductions are made to each account through the annual appropriations process each year. It is important to note, however, that these newly revised spending limits for each category would be enforced through a sequestration process, as explained in the "Statutory Limits on Discretionary Spending" section, above.

VOTE ON BALANCED BUDGET AMENDMENT TO THE CONSTITUTION

Requirement for Vote

Section 201 of the Budget Control Act states that the chambers "shall vote on passage of" a balanced budget amendment to the Constitution between September 30 and December 31, 2011.[97]

No requirements are placed on the specific content of the proposal to amend the Constitution. The BCA does not specify that the Senate must vote on a House-passed constitutional amendment, nor does it require that both chambers vote on the same constitutional amendment.

The BCA does not impose any procedural consequence if a chamber fails to vote on a balanced budget amendment. Factors besides procedure, however, might be expected to influence the decision to hold a vote. Furthermore, without successful final passage votes on the same measure in both chambers, the BCA precludes one avenue by which the debt limit may be increased by $1.5 trillion (instead of by $1.2 trillion). Specifically, if both chambers *approve* a Constitutional amendment by the required two-thirds vote, then the debt limit could be increased by $1.5 trillion; if one or both chambers do not approve a Constitutional amendment, then it can be increased only by $1.2 trillion. (Enactment of the joint committee bill is another avenue through which the debt limit could be increased by up to $1.5 trillion. See the section "Debt Ceiling Increase" above.)

The BCA does not establish any expedited procedures for initial consideration of a Constitutional amendment. If the House were to consider a House-originated Constitutional amendment, it would do so under its regular rules of procedure, possibly under the terms of a special rule or by a motion to suspend the rules. If the special rule permitted amendments they could be adopted by majority vote, but final adoption would require support from two-thirds of Members present and voting. If the Senate were to consider a Senate-originated Constitutional amendment, it also would do so under its regular rules. That would mean it would be brought to the floor by unanimous consent or a motion to proceed. The motion to proceed would be debatable, so bringing it to a vote might require a vote of three-fifths of the Senate to limit debate. The Constitutional amendment itself would also be debatable, which could again require cloture, and amendments could be offered and adopted by a majority of Senators present and voting, but the joint resolution could be agreed to only by two thirds of Senators present and voting.

Expedited Procedure for Consideration of Constitutional Amendment Approved by Other Chamber

Section 202 of the BCA establishes legislative procedures to expedite the consideration by one chamber of a joint resolution approved by the other. To be clear, these procedures will only be used if one chamber approves a Constitutional amendment with the required two-thirds vote. If that happens, then one chamber could use these procedures to consider a measure sent to it by the other.

The BCA provides that if the Senate receives a House-passed joint resolution, it will be referred to the committee of jurisdiction, which is required to report by the fifth session day after the Senate received the joint resolution from the House. If the committee does not report, it will be automatically discharged and the joint resolution will be placed on the calendar, making it eligible to be called up in the full Senate.

The Senate, however, must agree to take up the joint resolution under its regular rules, because the BCA does not affect the procedures for bringing the measure to the floor. The Senate could take up a House joint resolution by unanimous consent or by agreeing to a motion to proceed. While a simple majority could agree to a motion to proceed, the motion is debatable, and therefore the Senate might have to invoke cloture in order to get to a vote on the question of taking up the balanced budget amendment. Cloture requires the support of three-fifths of the Senate (normally 60 Senators) and several days to invoke.[98] As a result, Senators might not have the opportunity, however, of voting directly on the question of approving a House-passed balanced budget amendment. On the other hand, given that passage of the constitutional amendment has a higher threshold (two-thirds of those present and voting, normally 67 Senators) than cloture, any balanced budget amendment likely to be approved by the Senate could also likely clear this procedural hurdle.

If the Senate chooses to take up a House joint resolution proposing a balanced budget amendment then the BCA establishes special expedited procedures for the consideration of that joint resolution. The measure is to be considered for a total of 20 hours, including time spent in quorum calls and voting. The time would be equally divided between the majority and minority leaders or their designees. No Senator could offer an amendment to the joint resolution, and several other motions that would take the Senate off of consideration of the joint resolution are also precluded. If the Senate has voted to proceed to a House joint resolution, then the final passage vote is to occur immediately after the 20 hours is used or yielded back (except for one quorum call if requested) or no later than the seventh session day after the joint resolution was placed on the calendar.

The BCA also provides a special procedure the House could use to consider a Senate joint resolution proposing a balanced budget amendment, although the House might choose instead to consider the measure under the terms of a special rule or under suspension of the rules. To briefly summarize the special procedures, the BCA provides a method for a majority to take up a Senate-passed joint resolution on the floor and debate it for two hours, equally divided between those opposed and those in favor.[99] No amendments and no motion to recommit would be in order under the procedures for House consideration outlined in the BCA.

FEDERAL STUDENT AID PROGRAMS

The Budget Control Act of 2011 (BCA; P.L. 112-25) also makes changes to two of the federal student aid programs authorized under Title IV of the Higher Education Act of 1965, as amended (HEA; P.L. 89-329):

- The William D. Ford Federal Direct Loan (DL) program and
- The Federal Pell Grant program.

Federal Direct Loan Program (Student Loans)

The William D. Ford Federal Direct Loan (DL) program is the primary federal student loan program administered by the U.S. Department of Education (ED).[100] The program makes available loans to undergraduate and graduate students and the parents of dependent undergraduate students to help them finance their postsecondary education costs. Several types of loans are offered through the DL program: Subsidized Stafford Loans and Unsubsidized Stafford Loans for undergraduate, graduate, and professional students; PLUS Loans for graduate students and the parents of dependent undergraduate students; and Consolidation Loans through which borrowers may combine their loans into a single loan. The primary difference between Subsidized and Unsubsidized Stafford Loans is that with Unsubsidized Stafford Loans borrowers are responsible for paying the interest that accrues while they are in school, and during grace and deferment periods, whereas with Subsidized Stafford Loans the interest that accrues during these periods is paid by the government. DL program subsidy costs are mostly funded with mandatory appropriations, and administrative costs are mostly funded with discretionary appropriations.

The BCA eliminates the availability of Subsidized Stafford Loans to graduate and professional students for periods of instruction beginning on or after July 1, 2012, which corresponds to the beginning of award year 2012-13. After that date, graduate and professional students will be able to substitute amounts they previously would have been able to borrow using Subsidized Stafford Loans with Unsubsidized Stafford Loans. According to ED, during award year 2010-11, 1.47 million graduate and professional students borrowed $10.8 billion in Subsidized Stafford Loans; 1.34 million graduate and professional students borrowed $15.1 billion in Unsubsidized Stafford Loans;

and 0.34 million graduate and professional students borrowed $6.4 billion in PLUS Loans.

Also, effective for DL program loans first disbursed on or after July 1, 2012, the BCA eliminates the authority of the Secretary of Education to offer one of two repayment incentives to borrowers of DL program loans. At present, two types of repayment incentives are offered:

- Borrowers of Stafford Loans currently receive a 0.5% up-front interest rebate that partially offsets a 1% origination fee; and borrowers of PLUS Loans receive an up-front interest rebate of 1.5% that partially offsets a 4% origination fee. If a borrower who receives an up-front interest rebate fails to make the first 12 monthly loan payments on time, the rebated amount is added back to the borrower's loan principal, increasing the loan amount that must be repaid. The BCA eliminates authority for the Secretary to offer this benefit.
- Borrowers who repay DL program loans using automatic electronic debit currently receive a 0.25 percentage point reduction in their interest rate. The BCA retains authority for the Secretary to offer this benefit.

CBO estimates the changes in the DL program would reduce direct spending by $9.6 billion over the FY2012-FY2016 period and by $21.6 billion over the FY2012-FY2021 period. Approximately $17 billion of these savings would be directed to the Pell Grant program for future use, while $4.6 billion would go towards deficit reduction.[101]

Federal Pell Grant Program

The Federal Pell Grant program is the single largest source of federal grant aid supporting postsecondary education students.[102] The program provided over $34.7 billion to approximately 9.5 million undergraduate students in FY2010.[103]

The Pell Grant program is currently funded with three types of spending:

- Annual discretionary appropriations bills that provide most of the funding for the program and typically specify the base discretionary maximum grant level for the program in a given award year;

- Mandatory appropriations provided in "such sums as necessary" for the purposes of funding annual increases to the base discretionary maximum grant level each year, as specified in the HEA, under existing statutory parameters; and
- Additional specific amounts in mandatory appropriations provided in previous legislation[104] that are available for general use for a specific time period and may be used to pay for obligations associated with provisions that primarily affect discretionary spending in the program.

The BCA provides additional mandatory funding for the Pell Grant program for general use in FY2012 and FY2013, as depicted in the last category above. The BCA provides an additional $10 billion in mandatory funding for FY2012, and an additional $7 billion in mandatory funding for FY2013, for a total of an additional $17 billion.[105]

These additional appropriations would reduce the amount of discretionary appropriations required in FY2012 and FY2013. Despite the availability of the additional funds provided in the BCA, Congress would need to provide an additional $1.3 billion over the FY2011 discretionary funding amount to maintain the current award levels and eligibility parameters in FY2012.[106] Congress could also consider revising the program's award rules, eligibility parameters, and aid levels in order to reduce costs in the program, and therefore, reduce the amount of additional appropriations needed in FY2012. Other than providing additional mandatory funding, the BCA does not make any other changes to the Pell Grant program.

Appendix A. Frequently Asked Questions About the Budget Control Act

How Will the Spending Caps Affect a Specific Program (or Department or Agency)?

The effect of the limits placed on discretionary spending by the BCA on specific government programs, departments or agencies will be determined later through the regular appropriations process. The spending limits of the BCA are established for two broad categories for FY2012 and FY2013 ("security" and "nonsecurity") and for one overall discretionary category for

FY2014 through FY2021. Congress and the President will decide how to allocate spending within these constraints.

The BCA Authorized an Immediate Increase of the Federal Debt Ceiling. Are Subsequent Increases Contingent upon Congress Taking Any Other Action?

No. The BCA authorized an increase of the debt ceiling up to at least $2.1 trillion. If Congress does not take any other action, the increase up to $2.1 trillion will occur. Raising the debt ceiling to a higher level, up to a maximum of $2.4 trillion, is contingent on other action, namely the enactment of a joint committee bill that reduces the deficit by more than $1.2 trillion or the passage in both chambers of a balanced budget constitutional amendment. Furthermore, Congress can prevent subsequent stages of debt limit increases authorized by the BCA by enacting a "joint resolution of disapproval," a process expected to require support of two-thirds of each chamber to override a likely veto by the President.

Are there Any Content Requirements for the Joint Committee Bill to Be Considered under the Expedited Procedures?

To qualify as a joint committee bill under the definition in the BCA, the legislative language recommended by the Committee must include a statement of the deficit reduction achieved over the period of FY2012 to FY2021. Otherwise, the only other requirements the text must meet to be considered under the special procedures are (1) be recommended by a majority of joint committee members through a vote conducted on or before November 23, 2011; (2) be introduced by the House Speaker (or designee) the first legislative day after it is transmitted from the joint committee *or* be introduced by the Senate majority leader (or designee) the first day of session after it is transmitted from the joint committee; and (3) be passed by both chambers by December 23, 2011.

Can The Joint Committee Bill Contain Provisions Affecting Revenue?

Yes. The BCA does not contain any specific restrictions on the policy content of the joint committee bill. In order to comply with the Constitutional requirement that all bills affecting revenue originate in the House of Representatives, Section 402(e)(2) of the BCA ensures that the bill sent to the President for his signature will be the "H.R." version of the joint committee Bill, not the "S." version.

What Happens if the Joint Committee Bill Does Not Become Law?

If a joint committee bill reducing the deficit by at least $1.2 trillion over the period covering FY2012-FY2021 is not enacted by January 15, 2012, an automatic process to reduce spending will begin January 2, 2013. The spending reductions are achieved for direct spending through sequestration each year (FY2013 to FY2021). For discretionary spending, the reductions are achieved through sequestration the first year (FY2013). For the other fiscal years (FY2014- FY2021), the discretionary spending reductions are achieved through a downward adjustment of statutory limits on discretionary spending divided into two new categories that reflect defense and nondefense spending. Importantly, some programs, including both Social Security and Medicaid, are exempt from sequestration, and any sequestration of Medicare spending is capped at 2%.

If the Automatic Spending Reduction Process Occurs Because a Joint Committee Bill Does Not Become Law, How Much Will Spending Be Cut?

The amounts of spending reductions required each year cannot yet be known. It depends in part on the extent, if any, by which the reductions in the joint committee bill fall short of the $1.2 trillion goal and in part on spending estimates to be calculated in the future by the Office of Management and Budget (OMB). Furthermore, beginning in FY2014, part of the spending reductions will be achieved through a downward adjustment of the statutory limits on discretionary spending, not by automatic across-the-board spending cuts. For discretionary spending, it will therefore be Congress and the President who later determine the manner in which reductions are made to each account through the annual appropriations process each year.

What Programs and Activities Are Exempt from the Sequestration Process that Will Occur if a Joint Committee Bill Does Not Become Law?

The list of exempt programs and activities can be found in Section 255 of the Balanced Budget and Emergency Deficit Control Act, as amended (2 U.S.C. 905). The exempt programs include Social Security, Medicaid, and federal retirement and disability programs, among many others.

What Happens if a Balanced Budget Constitutional Amendment Is Not Sent to the States?

The BCA does not establish a procedural consequence if the House and Senate do not both pass a balanced budget constitutional amendment by the required two-thirds in each chamber. If the chambers do approve such a constitutional amendment, however, the BCA provides that the debt ceiling could be increased by $1.5 trillion, instead of by $1.2 trillion.

Do Both Chambers Have to Vote on a Balanced Budget Amendment?

Section 201 of the Budget Control Act states that the chambers "shall vote on passage of" a balanced budget amendment to the Constitution between September 30 and December 31, 2011. In the Senate, to get to a direct passage vote on a constitutional amendment, it might be necessary to secure support from 60 Senators to begin consideration of such a proposal. The BCA does not impose any procedural consequence if a chamber fails to vote on a balanced budget amendment. Factors besides procedure, however, might be expected to influence the decision to hold a vote. Without successful final passage votes on the same measure in both chambers, the BCA does preclude one avenue by which the debt limit may be increased by $1.5 trillion (instead of by $1.2 trillion).

Appendix B. Timelines for Actions in Expedited Procedures

Table B-1. Joint Committee on Deficit Reduction: Timeline for Actions

Date	Action and Provision of Law	Related Provisions
Not later than August 16, 2011	Appoint members and co-chairs of the joint committee (Section 401(b)(4)(D) and (Section 401(b)(4)C)(i))	
Not later than September 16, 2011	Hold first meeting of the joint committee (Section 401(b)(5)(E)(i))	
Not later than October 14, 2011	House and Senate standing committees submit recommendations to the joint committee (Section 401(b)(3)(ii))	
At least 48 hours prior to vote on joint committee report and proposal	CBO cost estimates must be available to joint committee members (Section 401(b)(5)(D)(ii))	
Not later than November 23, 2011	Joint committee votes on report and proposal (Section 401(b)(3)(B)(i))	If the committee does not vote by November 23, no legislation will be eligible for consideration under the expedited procedures of the BCA (Section 402 (g)(1))
"Promptly" after vote on joint committee report and proposal	Joint committee report, proposal, and record of vote to be made publicly available (Section 401(b)(3)(B)(v))	
No later than 3 days after vote on joint committee report and proposal	Submit any minority or alternative views for inclusion in the joint committee report (Section 401(b)(3)(B)(iii))	
Not later than December 2, 2011	Transmit joint committee report and proposal to the President, Vice President, House and Senate (Section 401(b)(3)(B)(iv))	
First legislative day after joint committee proposal is received	Introduce proposal in the form of a House bill (Section 402(a))	
First calendar day Senate is in session after joint committee proposal is received	Introduce proposal in the form of a Senate bill (Section 402(a))	
Not later than December 9, 2011	House committees report joint committee bill (Section 402(b)(1))	Motion to discharge a committee from consideration of bill is in order if it has not reported by December 9 (Section 402(b)(1))
Not later than December 9, 2011	Senate committees report joint committee	If any committee fails

Date	Action and Provision of Law	Related Provisions
	bill (Section 402(c)(1))	to report by December 9, it will be automatically discharged (Section 402(c)(1))
Not later than 2 days of session after date joint committee Bill is on Senate calendar	Senate majority leader can make motion to proceed to the joint committee bill (Section 402(c)(2))	If the joint committee bill has been on the calendar for two days of session, then any Senator can make a motion to proceed to its consideration (Section 402(c)(2))
Not later than December 23, 2011	Vote on final passage of the joint committee bill in both House and Senate (Section 402(b)(4) and Section 402(c)(5))	If vote on final passage does not occur by December 23, no legislation will be eligible for consideration under the expedited procedures of the BCA (Section 402 (g)(1))
By January 15, 2012	Joint committee bill enacted into law (Section 302(a))	If joint committee bill reducing deficit by at least $1.2 trillion is not enacted into law by January 15,
		sequestration will occur starting in 2013 (Section 302(a))
January 31, 2012	Joint committee is terminated (Section 401(d))	

Source: Budget Control Act of 2011, P.L. 112-25, see information in the table for specific citations to the act.

Table B-2. Dates for Introducing and Beginning Floor Consideration of Disapproval Resolutions, by Presidential Certification and Chamber

Date	Action and Provision of Law	Related Provisions
Senate disapproval resolution in response to first Presidential certification		
September 6, 7, 8, or 9 (or, if the Senate was not in session, the next calendar day on which the Senate is in session)	Introduction of joint resolution of disapproval (Section 301(b)(2)(A)(i))	
Immediately upon introduction of disapproval resolution	Disapproval resolution placed on the Senate calendar (Section 301(d)(2)	

Table B-2. (Continued)

Date	Action and Provision of Law	Related Provisions
From introduction until September 14, 2011	A non-debatable motion to proceed to the consideration of the disapproval resolution is in order (Section 301(d)(3)(A))	
House disapproval resolution in response to first Presidential certification		
September 6, 7, 8, or 9	Introduction of joint resolution of disapproval (Section 301(b)(2)(A)(i))	
Not later than 5 calendar days after introduction of disapproval resolution	Any committee of the House of Representatives to which the disapproval resolution is referred shall report it to the House without amendment (Section 301(c)(2))	If a committee fails to report the disapproval resolution within that period, the committee shall be discharged from considering it further and it will be referred to the appropriate calendar (Section 301(c)(2))
Not later than the sixth day after the introduction of the disapproval resolution	It shall be in order to move to proceed to consider the disapproval resolution (Section 301(c)(3))	
Senate disapproval resolution in response to second Presidential certification		
Between the date the certification is received and 3 calendar days after that date	Introduction of joint resolution of disapproval (Section 301(b)(2)(A)(ii))	If the Senate would otherwise not be in session in time to consider a joint resolution disapproving the second certification, the Senate majority leader (in consultation with the minority leader) is required to reconvene the Senate within two calendar days after receiving the certification from the President (Section 301(d)(1))
Immediately upon introduction of disapproval resolution	Disapproval resolution placed on the Senate calendar (Section 301(d)(2)	
From introduction until the 6th day after the date on which Congress receives a certification	A non-debatable motion to proceed to the consideration of the disapproval resolution is in order (Section 301(d)(3)(A))	
House disapproval resolution in response to second Presidential certification		
The day the certification was received or on any of the next 3 calendar days	Introduction of joint resolution of disapproval (Section 301(b)(2)(A)(ii))	If House would otherwise not be in session in time to

Date	Action and Provision of Law	Related Provisions
		consider a joint resolution disapproving the second certification, the House Speaker is required to reconvene the House within two calendar days after receiving the certification (Section 301(c)(1))
Not later than 5 calendar days after introduction of disapproval resolution	Any committee of the House of Representatives to which the disapproval resolution is referred is to report it to the House without amendment (Section 301(c)(2))	If a committee fails to report the disapproval resolution within that period, the committee shall be discharged from considering it further and it will be referred to the appropriate calendar (Section 301(c)(2))
Not later than the sixth day after the introduction of the disapproval resolution	It shall be in order to move to proceed to consider the disapproval resolution (Section 301(c)(3))	

Source: Budget Control Act of 2011, P.L. 112-25, see information in the table for specific citations to the act.

Notes: Under the Budget Control Act of 2011, the President submitted to Congress a certification that the debt subject to limit was within $100 billion of the debt limit on August 2, 2011, and this is identified as the "first" certification in the table. If the debt limit has been increased by $900 billion, the President may submit another certification when the debt subject to limit is within $100 billion of the debt limit, and this is identified as the "second" certification in the table.

End Notes

[1] For more information, see CRS Report RL31967, *The Debt Limit: History and Recent Increases*, by D. Andrew Austin and Mindy R. Levit; and CRS Report R41633, *Reaching the Debt Limit: Background and Potential Effects on Government Operations*, coordinated by Mindy R. Levit.

[2] President Obama submitted such certification on August 2, 2011. It is available at http://www.whitehouse.gov/thepress-office/2011/08/02/message-president-us-congress.

[3] For information on the projected savings and impact on budget deficit projections resulting from these limits, see Congressional Budget Office, Letter to Honorable John A. Boehner, Speaker, U.S. House of Representatives, and Honorable Harry Reid, majority leader, United

States Senate, cost estimate of the Budget Control Act of 2011, as posted on the website of the House Committee on Rules, August 1, 2011.

[4] Section 251(b)(2)(A) of the Balanced Budget and Emergency Deficit Control Act of 1985 (BBEDCA), as amended by the BCA, provides for the caps to be adjusted for any discretionary appropriations designated as "for Overseas Contingency Operations/Global War on Terrorism."

[5] See, for example, Lori Montgomery, "Obama signs debt bill after Senate passage," *Washington Post*, August 3, 2011, p. A1; Joseph J. Schatz and Alan K. Ota, "Deal Reached to Boost Debt Limit, Cut Deficit," *CQ Today Online News*, July 31, 2011; and Fawn Johnson, Chris Strohm, and Coral Davenport, et al., "The Debt Deal: Issue by Issue," *National Journal Daily*, August 1, 2011.

[6] For information on proposals to amend the Constitution to require that the federal budget be balanced, see CRS Report R41907, *A Balanced Budget Constitutional Amendment: Background and Congressional Options* , by James V. Saturno and Megan Suzanne Lynch.

[7] For a description of the Federal Pell Grant program, see CRS Report R41437, *Federal Pell Grant Program of the* description of the DL program, see CRS Report R40122, *Federal Student Loans Made Under the Federal Family Education Loan Program and the William D. Ford Federal Direct Loan Program: Terms and Conditions for Borrowers*, by David P. Smole.

[8] See also CRS Report 98-888, *"Fast-Track" or Expedited Procedures: Their Purposes, Elements, and Implications*, by Christopher M. Davis

[9] Article 1, Section 5.

[10] Section 301 (g)(2), with respect to consideration of a joint resolution disapproving a debt limit increase, and Section 404(2), with respect to the Joint Committee bill, state that the provisions are enacted by Congress with "full recognition of the constitutional right of either House to change the rules (so far as relating to the procedure of the House) at any time, in the same manner, and to the same extent as the case of any other rule of that House."

[11] President Obama submitted such certification on August 2, 2011. It is available at http://www.whitehouse.gov/thepress-office/2011/08/02/message-president-us-congress.

[12] Sequestration is a process of automatic largely across-the-board spending cuts to non-exempt programs. Under the specified procedures, the cuts would be equally split between defense and non-defense nonexempt programs. For background information on the sequestration process, see CRS Report R41901, *Statutory Budget Controls in Effect Between 1985 and 2002*, by Megan Suzanne Lynch.

[13] The debt limit increase would be equal to the amount by which the legislation reduces the deficit, if such amount exceeds $1.2 trillion, up to $1.5 trillion.

[14] Section 301(b)(2)(D).

[15] The BCA provides that if the Senate is not in session on any of those days, the joint resolution will qualify for expedited consideration if it is introduced the next calendar day after September 9, 2011 that the Senate is in session.

[16] If no Senator introduces a joint resolution of disapproval, and the House passes one, then the House-passed joint resolution is to be eligible for Senate consideration under the expedited procedures.

[17] Regular Senate rules provide a means for a single Senator to cause a measure to be placed directly on the calendar, but it takes several legislative days. For more information, see CRS Report RS22299, *Bypassing Senate Committees: Rule XIV and Unanimous Consent*, by Michael L. Koempel.

[18] More specifically, for the joint resolution of disapproval that must be introduced between September 6 and 9 (or, if the Senate is not in session those days, the next calendar day after September 9 that it is in session), the non-debatable motion to proceed is in order from the time of introduction until September 14, 2011, or a maximum of 8 days after introduction. For the joint resolution to disapprove the second debt limit increase, the non-debatable motion to proceed is in order from the time of the joint resolution's introduction (which can occur the day the certification is received or on any of the next 3 calendar days) until the sixth day after the certification is received, or a maximum of 6 days after introduction.

[19] Under Section 301(d)(3)(A) of the BCA, the motion to proceed to a joint resolution of disapproval can be made "Notwithstanding Rule XXII" (the cloture rule). Presumably, a motion to proceed could be made even if the Senate was considering another matter on which cloture had been invoked, something otherwise barred by Rule XXII.

[20] Section 301(d)(3)(A).

[21] Presumably, the time used for votes and the time used for quorum calls will be charged equally to each side.

[22] Section 301(d)(3)(C).

[23] To prevent questions already decided by the House from being re-visited, once a motion to proceed has been disposed of, another motion to proceed is not in order. In addition, motions to reconsider the question of taking up the joint resolution or the question on passage are not in order.

[24] For more information, see CRS Report 98-383, *Motions to Recommit in the House*, by Betsy Palmer.

[25] Section 301(f)(4)(B).

[26] See CRS Report RS22654, *Veto Override Procedure in the House and Senate*, by Elizabeth Rybicki.

[27] After 10 days, if Congress is in session, the measure would become law without the President's signature. If Congress has ended its session and the President does not sign the measure, it will not become law; this action is known as a "pocket veto." For more information, see CRS Report RS22188, *Regular Vetoes and Pocket Vetoes: An Overview*, by Kevin R. Kosar.

[28] There is apparent ambiguity with regard to how days in which either house is not in session are to be counted. Section 301(b)(1) states that the 50 days and 15 days run "(regardless of whether Congress is in session)." Section 301(f)(4) states that the period beginning from presentation and ending the date the President "signs, allows to become law without his signature, or vetoes and returns the joint resolution (but excluding days when either House is not in session) shall be disregarding in computing the appropriate calendar day period...."

[29] Discretionary spending represents a portion of total federal spending. The other portion, referred to as direct spending (also referred to as mandatory spending), is generally provided in or controlled by authorizing legislation that requires federal payments to individuals or entities, often based on eligibility criteria and benefit formulas set forth in statute. Some direct spending is funded in appropriations acts, referred to as appropriated entitlements, but is controlled by the authorizing statute(s). Direct spending, including direct spending provided in appropriations acts, is not subject to the statutory limits.

[30] For further information, see CRS Report R41901, *Statutory Budget Controls in Effect Between 1985 and 2002*, by Megan Suzanne Lynch.

[31] For information on the projected savings and impact on budget deficit projections resulting from these limits, see Congressional Budget Office, Letter to Honorable John A. Boehner, Speaker, U.S. House of Representatives, and Honorable Harry Reid, majority leader, United

States Senate, cost estimate of the Budget Control Act of 2011, August 1, 2011, available at http://www.cbo.gov/doc.cfm?index=12357.

[32] Previous discretionary limits under the BEA, as extended through FY2002, also allowed for specific adjustments.

[33] Any adjustment is based on the designation, not on the purpose for which the appropriations are provided. That is, Congress and the President may designate any appropriations as emergency requirements or for OCO/GWOT, as they so choose. Section 102 of the BCA defines in statute, by amending the BBEDCA, the term "emergency." However, this definition is not directly tied to the designation for purposes of any adjustments to the statutory limits on discretionary spending.

[34] For further information on such initiatives, see CRS Report RL34217, *Medicare Program Integrity: Activities to Protect Medicare from Payment Errors, Fraud, and Abuse*, by Cliff Binder.

[35] "Disaster relief" is defined as "activities carried out pursuant to a determination under Section 102(2) of the Robert T. Stafford Disaster Relief and Emergency Assistance Act (42 U.S.C. 5122(2))." Appropriations for such "disaster relief" may not be designated as emergency requirements or for OCO/GWOT. Within 30 days of enactment of the BCA, OMB is required to report to the Committee on Appropriations and Budget of each House the average funding provided for disaster relief.

[36] Under Section 258(b) of the BBEDCA, as restored by the repeal of the expiration date in Section 104 of the BCA, the sequestration process is suspended upon the enactment of a declaration of war.

[37] "Budgetary resources" include new budget authority, unobligated balances, and obligation limitations. Certain programs and budget accounts are exempt from any sequestration, such as all programs administered by the Department of Veterans Affairs, as provided by Section 255 of the BBEDCA (as restored by Section 104 of the BCA). In addition, the President may exempt any military personnel account or provide for a lower uniform percentage reduction in any such account, provided that he notify Congress of such actions by August 10 and, if a sequestration is required, that other accounts in budget subfunctional category 051 ("Department of Defense-Military") be reduced by a uniform percentage to offset the amount not reduced by such exemption.

[38] Section 258A of the BBEDCA provides expedited procedures in the Senate for a joint resolution modifying a final sequestration order.

[39] If a budget account has received only a part-year appropriation at the time of the sequestration order, in a continuing appropriations act, for example, the reduction is taken from the annualized amount of the part-year appropriation, and from the full-year amount, when a full-year appropriation is enacted.

[40] The BCA amends Section 314(a) of the Budget Act to allow the chairs of the Budget Committee of each house to make the adjustments provided under the new Section 251 of the BBEDCA, as described above.

[41] Generally, the primary procedural constraint on the level of discretionary spending provided in appropriations acts is the point of order enforcing the Section 302(b) allocations associated with the congressional budget resolution. To the extent the levels of discretionary spending included in the congressional budget resolution for a fiscal year are consistent with the statutory caps for that year, the Section 302(b) allocations will continue to be the primary procedural enforcement of discretionary spending levels. For additional information on the suballocations, see CRS Report RS20144, *Allocations and Subdivisions in the Congressional Budget Process*, by Bill Heniff Jr.

[42] An appeal from the ruling of the chair on such a point of order requires only a majority vote. However, this point of order is duplicative of the point of order under Section 312(b) of the Budget Act, which requires an affirmative vote of three-fifths of Senators for a motion to waive the point of order and for an appeal from the decision of the chair.

[43] Many of these reports are required by Section 254 of the BBEDCA, which was restored by Section 104 of the BCA.

[44] In addition, if a supplemental appropriations act is enacted before July 1 and would cause a spending limit to be breached, OMB would be required to issue a within-session sequestration report 15 days after the enactment of the appropriation.

[45] Section 104(b) of the CBA relieved CBO from issuing a sequestration preview report.

[46] Specifically, it amends Section 314 of the Budget Act.

[47] The new section specifies that such rules would also apply to a provision "reducing revenue" designated as an emergency requirement. However, Section 251(b)(2)(A) of the BBEDCA, as amended by the BCA, pertains to discretionary appropriations so designated only; that is, presumably a provision reducing revenue could not be designated as an emergency requirement pursuant to Section 251(b)(2)(A) of the BBEDCA. Therefore, it is unclear how this new provision would affect legislation reducing revenue. In addition, the BCA appears to restate Section 314(d)(1) in a new Section 314(d)(2)(A); the only difference is that Section 314(d)(2)(A)refers to "a designation ... as an emergency pursuant to paragraph (1)," which is Section 314(d)(1). Therefore, this second provision presumably would have no additional effect.

[48] The BCA also amended Section 314(a) of the Budget Act to allow the chair of the House Committee on the Budget to "make appropriate budgetary adjustments of new budget authority and the outlays flowing therefrom in the same amount as required by section 251(b) of the [BBEDCA]." "Appropriate budget adjustments" might include the amounts included in, and associated with, the congressional budget resolution, which are enforced under Titles III and IV of the Budget Act. Presumably, the chair would not make such adjustments if the budgetary effects were not counted as provided under Section 314(d)(1).

[49] There appears to be some ambiguity in the plain text of the rule as to an applicable "designation." The rule specifies "a designation under subparagraph (A)" (i.e., Section 314(d)(2)(A) of the Budget Act), which refers to "a designation pursuant to paragraph (1)" (i.e., Section 314(d)(1) of the Budget Act). Section 314(d)(1) does not appear to confer any authority to designate a provision as an emergency; instead, the section, as noted above, requires that the budgetary effects of a provision designated as an emergency requirement pursuant to Section 251(b)(2)(A) of the BBEDCA not be counted for purposes of certain budget constraints.

[50] For further information on spending allocations under the Budget Act, see CRS Report RS20144, *Allocations and Subdivisions in the Congressional Budget Process*, by Bill Heniff Jr.

[51] For further information on general restrictions on amendments in the House, see CRS Report 98-995, *The Amending Process in the House of Representatives*, by Christopher M. Davis.

[52] The provisions are similar to so-called "deeming resolution" provisions that the Senate and the House have adopted individually in the absence of an agreement on a budget resolution. For more information on such "deeming resolutions," see CRS Report RL31443, *The "Deeming Resolution": A Budget Enforcement Tool*, by Megan Suzanne Lynch.

[53] Once filed, the budget levels presumably will also be submitted for printing in the *Congressional Record.*

[54] The chair may also adjust such levels pursuant to the adjustments allowed under the BCA, such as the adjustment for appropriations designated for Overseas Contingency Operations/Global War on Terrorism. In addition, Section 106(d)(2) of the BCA provides that Sections 412 (relating to administrative expenses of the Social Security Administration and of the Postal Service), 413 (relating to the application and effect of such adjustments), and 414 (providing authority to make adjustments to reflect changes in concepts and definitions) of S.Con.Res. 13, the FY2010 budget resolution, shall remain in effect.

[55] The Senate PAYGO rule is provided in Section 201 of S.Con.Res. 13 (110th Congress), the FY2008 budget resolution. For further information on the Senate PAYGO rule, see CRS Report RL31943, *Budget Enforcement Procedures: Senate Pay-As-You-Go (PAYGO) Rule*, by Bill Heniff Jr.

[56] The Members of the House appointed to the joint committee are Jeb Hensarling (R-TX), co-chair; Dave Camp (RMI); Fred Upton (R-MI); Xavier Becerra (D-CA); James E. Clyburn (D-SC); and Chris Van Hollen (D-MD). The Senators appointed to the joint committee are Patty Murray (D-WA), co-chair; Max Baucus (D-MT); John F. Kerry (DMA); Jon Kyl (R-AZ); Rob Portman (R-OH); and Patrick J. Toomey (R-PA).

[57] For more information regarding Senate Ethics, see http://ethics.senate.gov/downloads/pdffiles/manual.pdf. For more information regarding House Ethics, see http://ethics.house.gov/Default.aspx.

[58] This section authored by Ida A. Brudnick, Analyst on the Congress. Questions concerning congressional staff and funding for the committee should be directed to her at 7-6460.

[59] Section 401(c)(1). These may include, for example, rules and laws pertaining to pay ceilings, pay dates, the Congressional Accountability Act, financial disclosure, gifts, conflicts of interest, and political activities. For additional information, see the Senate Rules at http://rules.senate.gov/public/index.cfm?p=RulesOfSenateHome, and the Senate Ethics Manual at http://ethics.senate.gov/downloads/pdffiles/manual.pdf.

[60] Section 401(c)(2). For more information regarding Senate Ethics see http://ethics.senate.gov/downloads/pdffiles/manual.pdf. For more information regarding House Ethics, see http://ethics.house.gov/Default.aspx

[61] Section 401(b)(5)(G).

[62] Section 401(b)(5)(B). This section refers to authorized expenses of the Joint Economic Committee under 15 U.S.C. 1024(d), which addresses the employment and compensation of personnel; cost of stenographic services; and utilization of Government services and private research agencies.

[63] Section 401(b)(3)(B)(i).

[64] Under Section 401(b)(3)(B), any change to House Rules or the Standing Rules of the Senate proposed in either the report or the legislative language "shall be considered as merely advisory."

[65] Section 401(a)(3)(B)(v).

[66] House Rule X, clause 10(b) requires that any joint committee comply with House Rule XI, clause 2(a).

[67] Clause 2(a) of House Rule XI (which Rule X(10)(b) appears to require to apply to joint committees) states that standing committee rules may not be inconsistent with House rules and directs standing committees to incorporate all of House Rule XI, clause 2 into committee rules "to the extent applicable." Clause 2 of House Rule XI requires that, among other things, meetings be open to the public and that a committee keep a substantially verbatim account of its proceedings.

[68] The BCA provides that if a bill is not introduced or considered in the Senate, and if the House has passed a Joint Committee bill, then that House-passed bill can be considered in the Senate under the expedited procedures described in the act (Section 402 (f)(1)).

[69] Regular Senate procedures provide a method for any single Senator, by taking certain actions on different days in the Senate, to have a bill or joint resolution placed directly on the calendar instead of being referred to committee. For a full explanation, see CRS Report RS22299, *Bypassing Senate Committees: Rule XIV and Unanimous Consent*, by Michael L. Koempel.

[70] Ordinarily, legislative days coincide with calendar days that the House is in session. A "legislative day" begins when the House convenes after an adjournment and ends when the House adjourns.

[71] For more information, see CRS Report RL30360, *Filibusters and Cloture in the Senate*, by Richard S. Beth, Valerie Heitshusen, and Betsy Palmer.

[72] More specifically, consideration of the Joint Committee bill could begin either when the motion to proceed was made and agreed to by voice vote or when the Senate agreed to take up the measure by unanimous consent.

[73] Section 402(c)(2).

[74] The BCA also makes in order a nondebatable motion to further limit debate on the joint committee bill, which requires a three-fifths vote for approval (normally 60 Senators). The time spent considering the bill could also be less than 30 hours if Senators controlling time "yield back" time or if the Senate modifies the terms of consideration by unanimous consent.

[75] It *would not* operate the way the time limitation works on consideration of a budget resolution or budget reconciliation bill. In both of those cases, the time limit is on "debate," not "consideration," so that at the conclusion of the statutory time limit it is still possible to offer (but not debate) amendments and other motions. This can lead to what has been termed a "vote-a-rama," when the Senate votes on amendments one after another, with a discussion of the amendment (usually just two minutes of it) allowed only by unanimous consent. For more information see CRS Memorandum to the Senate Budget Committee, "Budget Resolutions and Reconciliation Legislation in Calendar Years 1987-2008: Amendments Considered Before and After the Statutory Limit on Debate Expired," by Bill Heniff Jr. (U.S. Congress, Senate Committee on the Budget, *Senate Procedures for Consideration of the Budget Resolution/Reconciliation*, 110th Cong., 1st sess., February 12, 2009, S.Hrg. 111-106 (Washington: GPO, 2009), pp. 42-62.) (Memorandum is also available at Senate Budget Committee website, http://budget.senate.gov/democratic/.)

[76] The Budget Control Act does not specify how time used for quorum calls or voting would be charged. Because the BCA states that the 30 hours "shall be equally divided between the majority and minority leaders or their designees" (Section 401(c)(3)), one possible interpretation is that the time used for votes and the time for quorum calls will be charged equally to each side. Under the precedents of the Senate, if the absence of a quorum is suggested when the Senate is operating under time controlled pursuant to a unanimous consent agreement, the time consumed by the quorum call is charged against the side noting the absence of a quorum (Floyd M. Riddick and Alan S. Frumin, *Riddick's Senate Procedure: Precedents and Practices*, 101st Cong., 2nd sess., S. Doc. 101-28 (Washington: GPO, 1992), [Hereafter *Riddick's Senate Procedure*], p. 1066). This is also how time for quorum calls is charged when legislation is being considered under the Budget Act of 1974 (e.g., a budget resolution or a reconciliation bill). In both cases, unanimous consent is often

obtained to charge the time equally to both sides. Under the Budget Act of 1974, time spent voting is not charged against the debate time provided.

[77] Section 402(c)(5)and Section 402(g)(2) of the BCA.

[78] If the committees are discharged not through the BCA privileged motion but through the regular discharge process, the same proceedings apply as if the measure was reported. For more information on the House discharge rule, see CRS Report 98-394, *Discharge Procedure in the House*, by Richard S. Beth.

[79] For more information, see CRS Report 98-383, *Motions to Recommit in the House*, by Betsy Palmer.

[80] Section 402(b)(4) and Section 402(g)(2) of the BCA.

[81] Section 404(2) of the Budget Control Act specifically states that the procedures are established "with full recognition of the constitutional right of either House to change such rules (so far as relating to such House) at any time, in the same manner, and to the same extent as in the case of any other rule of such House." A special rule is one of the common ways in which the House implements this constitutional power.

[82] The Rules Committee could report a special rule permitting amendments to the Joint Committee bill. Presumably, however, the amended legislation would not be eligible for expedited consideration in the Senate, as it would fail to meet the definition of "Joint Committee Bill" in Section 401(a)(2), "a bill consisting of the proposed legislative language of the joint committee" recommended and introduced pursuant to the BCA.

[83] House Rule XIII, clause 6(c) prohibits the Rules Committee from reporting most resolutions that would prevent a motion to recommit a bill or joint resolution offered by the minority leader or his designee. In the case of a Joint Committee bill, however, a reference to the statutory prohibition in the special rule could prevent the motion to recommit without violating House Rule XIII, clause 6(c) . For example, special rules for trade agreement implementation bills in recent Congresses have prohibited the motion to recommit by stating that "Pursuant to" the relevant section of the Trade Act of 1974, the previous question shall be considered as ordered on the bill to final passage without intervening motion. See H.Res. 801, 110th Congress; H.Res. 386, H.Res. 583, and H.Res. 925, 109th Congress; and H.Res. 329, H.Res. 712, and H.Res. 738,108th Congress.

[84] See CRS Report RS22654, *Veto Override Procedure in the House and Senate*, by Elizabeth Rybicki.

[85] Section 302 of the BCA amends the Balanced Budget and Emergency Deficit Control Act (BBEDCA) by adding a new Section 251A.

[86] For the purposes of the following explanation and this report, it is assumed that the new spending limits will be applied using the definitions of "revised security category" and "revised nonsecurity category" in section 251A(1). The plain text of the statute, however, omits the term "revised" from the provisions of section 251A(2), using instead the terms "security category" and "nonsecurity category." As a result, it may be possible to question whether the discretionary spending limits required by section 251A will, if necessary, actually be applied in a manner consistent with the provision's apparent goals.

[87] For a brief description of the budget functional categories, see CRS Report 98-280, *Functional Categories of the Federal Budget*, by Bill Heniff Jr. For further information, see Government Accountability Office, *Budget Function Classifications: Origins, Trends, and Implications for Current Uses*, GAO/AIMD-98-67, February 1998.

[88] As noted, OMB is tasked with this calculation, and therefore, it appears that OMB would have sole responsibility in determining the amount of deficit reduction achieved in the Joint Committee bill, if enacted. However, Section 401(b)(3)(B)(i)(II) of the BCA requires that

the bill itself include a statement of deficit reduction. While the BCA does not explicitly require OMB to use this statement in determining the amount of deficit reduction achieved by the bill, OMB could use it by choice, or the statement in the bill could be written explicitly to require OMB to use it. If the statement does not include such a specific requirement and OMB itself determines the amount of deficit reduction achieved in the bill, presumably it would make such determination in relation to the baseline as calculated under Section 257 of the BBEDCA, which prescribes generally a current-law baseline. For a brief description of baselines in the budget process, see CRS Report 98-560, *Baselines and Scorekeeping in the Federal Budget Process*, by Bill Heniff Jr.

89 In order to determine the proportions, the calculation specified in the BCA uses the revised spending limits for discretionary spending and the OMB's baseline level of nonexempt accounts for direct spending. That is, the discretionary spending amount apparently includes programs and accounts exempt from any sequestration, while the direct spending amount does not. In addition, it is unclear whether the revised spending limit used in the calculation would include the adjustments provided for in Section 251(b) of the BBEDCA, as amended by the BCA (e.g., for discretionary appropriation for Overseas Contingency Operations/Global War on Terrorism). While the formula in the act does not explicitly specify whether or not the adjustments are included, the calculations are made on a date after which the adjustments would have been made to the limits (January 2, 2013, for FY2013, and when the sequestration preview reports are issued, for FY2014-FY2021).

90 The amounts are calculated at the beginning of each year. Therefore, the amounts for each of the four categories may not be the same for each year because the proportions between discretionary and direct spending within each category, especially the nondefense category, may change. For example, if discretionary appropriations decline as a proportion of nondefense spending, then the amount of reductions required in discretionary appropriations will decline.

91 The sequestration process was first established in 1985 by the Balanced Budget and Emergency Deficit Control Act (Title II of P.L. 99-177), commonly known as the Gramm-Rudman-Hollings Act. Initially, the sequestration process was tied to annual maximum deficit targets, declining to zero by a date certain, established by the law. If the budget deficit exceeded those target levels (plus a margin-of-error amount in some years), automatic across-the-board spending cuts would be triggered. The process was intended to provide an incentive to Congress and the President to reduce the deficit through legislative action to avoid an automatic sequestration. Since then, the law has been amended and modified several times. Notably, the Budget Enforcement Act (BEA) of 1990 (title XIII of P.L. 101-508) changed the focus of the sequestration process. Instead of maximum deficit targets, the BEA of 1990 tied sequestration to new statutory spending limits and PAYGO rules. The change was intended to hold Congress and the President accountable for projected budget outcomes that would result from new legislation, rather than the level of the deficit which could be affected by factors beyond their direct control, such as economic growth, inflation, and demographic changes. Most recently, prior to the enactment of the BCA, the Statutory Pay-As-You-Go Act of 2010 (Title I of P.L. 111-139) amended the BBEDCA to tie sequestration to a revised PAYGO rule. For further information on the legislative history of the sequestration process, see CRS Report R41901, *Statutory Budget Controls in Effect Between 1985 and 2002*, by Megan Suzanne Lynch, and CRS Report R41157, *The Statutory Pay-As-You-Go Act of 2010: Summary and Legislative History*, by Bill Heniff Jr. (The latter report was written by former CRS Specialist Robert Keith.)

[92] "Budgetary resources" include new budget authority, unobligated balances, direct spending authority, and obligation limitations, as defined in Section 250(c)(6) of the BBEDCA.

[93] Because the BCA is an amendment to the BBEDCA, and because it repeals the BBEDCA's expiration date, it would appear that the exemptions provided in Section 255 of the BBEDCA would apply to any sequestration order. The BCA explicitly indicates as much in relation to the sequestration process involving direct spending, but does not do so explicitly in relation to the sequestration process involving discretionary appropriations. This different treatment in the legislative language of the BCA may raise some questions about whether or not any discretionary appropriations were intended to be exempted from the sequestration process.

[94] In addition, the President may exempt any military personnel account or provide for a lower uniform percentage reduction in any such account, provided that he notify Congress of such actions by August 10 and, if a sequestration is required, that other accounts in budget subfunctional category 051 ("Department of Defense-Military") are reduced by a uniform percentage to offset the amount not reduced.

[95] On such dates, OMB is also required to provide a report to Congress containing information on the calculations, the adjusted discretionary spending limits, the reductions in nonexempt direct spending accounts, and any other appropriate information.

[96] In addition, under Section 256(k)(2) of the BBEDCA, the uniform percentage reduction is applied to all programs, projects, and activities within a budget account, as delineated, for accounts included in appropriations acts, in those acts or accompanying reports, and, for accounts not included in appropriations acts, in the most recently submitted President's budget.

[97] For information on the issue of amending the Constitution to require that the budget of the federal government be balanced, see CRS Report R41907, *A Balanced Budget Constitutional Amendment: Background and Congressional Options* , by James V. Saturno and Megan Suzanne Lynch.

[98] For more information on the cloture process, see CRS Report RL30360, *Filibusters and Cloture in the Senate*, by Richard S. Beth, Valerie Heitshusen, and Betsy Palmer.

[99] The Senate joint resolution is to be referred to the Committee on the Judiciary, and if the committee has not reported within five legislative days, a motion to discharge the committee is in order and debatable for 20 minutes, equally divided between a proponent and an opponent. If the motion to discharge is agreed to, the House would proceed immediately to consideration of the Joint Committee bill.

[100] For a description of the DL program, see CRS Report R40122, *Federal Student Loans Made Under the Federal Family Education Loan Program and the William D. Ford Federal Direct Loan Program: Terms and Conditions for Borrowers*, by David P. Smole.

[101] CBO Analysis of the FY2011 Budget Control Act, *Letter to Hon. John Boehner and Hon. Harry Reid*, dated August 1, 2011. See http://www.cbo.gov/ftpdocs/123xx/doc 12357/ BudgetControlActAug1.pdf.

[102] For a description of the Federal Pell Grant program, see CRS Report R41437, *Federal Pell Grant Program of the Higher Education Act: Background, Recent Changes, and Current Legislative Issues*, by Shannon M. Mahan.

[103] Taken from data available online from the U.S. Department of Education at http://federalstudentaid.ed.gov/datacenter/programmatic.html.

[104] For example, $13.5 billion in additional mandatory appropriations were provided for general use in the program for FY2011 in the SAFRA Act, passed as part of the Health Care and Education Reconciliation Act of 2010 (HCERA; P.L. 111-152).

[105] Per the HEA, these funds are available on October 1 of each applicable fiscal year and remain available through the end of each succeeding fiscal year. For example, the additional $10 billion provided for FY2012 will be available for use between October 1, 2011 and September 30, 2013.

[106] Based on estimates provided by CBO in April 2011.

In: The Budget Control Act of 2011
Editors: C. G. Lynch and C. McHale
ISBN: 978-1-61942-035-9

Chapter 2

CBO ANALYSIS OF THE BUDGET CONTROL ACT*

Congressional Budget Office

Douglas W. Elmendorf, Director
U.S. Congress
Washington, DC 20515

August 1, 2011

Honorable John A. Boehner
Speaker
U.S. House of Representatives
Washington, DC 20515

Honorable Harry Reid
Majority Leader
United States Senate
Washington, DC 20510

* This is an edited, reformatted and augmented version of a Congressional Budget Office publication, on Analysis of the Budget Control Act, dated August 1, 2011.

Dear Mr. Speaker and Mr. Leader:

The Congressional Budget Office has estimated the impact on the deficit of the Budget Control Act of 2011, as posted on the Web site of the House Committee on Rules on August 1, 2011. The legislation would:

- Establish caps on discretionary spending through 2021;
- Allow for certain amounts of additional spending for "program integrity" initiatives aimed at reducing the amount of improper benefit payments;
- Make changes to the Pell Grant and student loan programs;
- Require that the House of Representatives and the Senate vote on a joint resolution proposing a balanced budget amendment to the Constitution;
- Establish a procedure to increase the debt limit by $400 billion initially and procedures that would allow the limit to be raised further in two additional steps, fo r a cumul ative increase of between $2.1 trillion and $2.4 trillion;
- Reinstate and modify certain budget process rules;
- Create a Congressional Joint Select Committee on Deficit Reduction to propose fu rther defi cit reduction, with a stated goal of achieving at least $1.5 trillion in b udgetary s avings over 10 years; and
- Establish automatic procedures for reducing spending by as much as $1.2 trillion if legislation originating with the new joint select committee does not achieves uch savings.

If appropriations in the next 10 years are equal to the caps on discretionary spending and the maximum amount of funding is provided for the program integrity initiatives, CBO estimates that the legislation—apart from the provisions related to the joint select committee—would reduce budget deficits by $917 billion between 2012 and 2021. In addition, legislation originating with the joint select committee, or the automatic reductions in spending that would occur in the absence of such legislation, would reduce deficits by at least $1.2 trillion over the 10-year period. Therefore, the deficit reduction stemming from this legislation would total at least $2.1 trillion over the 2012-202 1 period.

Those amounts are relative to CBO's March 2011 baseline adjusted for subsequent appropriation action. CBO has also calculated the net budgetary impact if discretionary savings are measured relative to its January baseline projections. Relative to that baseline, CBO estimates that the legislation would reduce budget deficits by at least $2.3 trillion between 2012 and 2021.

DISCRETIONARY CAPS

The August 1, 2011, version of the Budget Control Act of 2011 would impose caps on appropriations of new discretionary budget authority that start at $1,043 billion in 2012 and reach $1,234 billion in 2021. For 2012 and 2013, separate caps for "security" and "nonsecurity" budget authority would be in effect; from 2014 on, only one cap would apply to total discretionary funding.[1]

The caps would not apply to spending for the wars in Afghanistan and Iraq and for similar activities (sometimes referred to as overseas contingency operations) or to certain amounts of additional spending for "program integrity" initiatives, for which the act would allow upward adjustments to the caps by specified amounts. In addition, the legislation provides for adjustments to the caps in each fiscal year to account for funding designated for emergency requirements and disaster relief. The cap adjustments for disaster relief would be limited to amounts based on historical averages for such funding.

In Table 1, CBO compares estimated spending under the caps to two projections of discretionary spending:

- CBO's March 2011 baseline, with two adjustments: (1) excluding spending associated with overseas contingency operations—that is, excluding spending that was projected by assuming that the amount of funding provided in 2011 for the wars in Afghanistan and Iraq would continue to be provided for similar activities in future years, with adjustments for inflation; and (2) incorporating the effect of full-year appropriations for 2011, which were enacted after that baseline was completed.
- CBO's January 2011 baseline excluding spending that was projected by assuming that the amount of funding provided in 2011 for the wars in Afghanistan and Iraq would continue to be provided for similar activities in future years, with adjustments for inflation.

In CBO's baseline projections, appropriations for discretionary programs are assumed to grow each year with inflation from the amounts provided for the most recent year. The March baseline, as adjusted, incorporates reductions in projected spending resulting from appropriation actions that occurred after the January baseline had been prepared. In particular, the Department of Defense and Full-Year Continuing Appropriations Act, 2011 (P.L. 112-10) established discretionary funding levels for the current year, while the earlier January baseline reflected funding levels that were largely a temporary extension of the 2010 appropriations.

Relative to the adjusted March baseline, proposed budget authority would be $840 billion lower and outlays would be $756 billion lower over the 2012-2021 period. Relative to the January baseline, excluding funding for the wars in Iraq and Afghanistan and for similar activities, the proposed caps would lower budget authority by nearly $1.1 trillion and outlays by $935 billion over the 2012-2021 period (see Table 1). The projected reductions in outlays are smaller than the projected reductions in budget authority because outlays generally lag behind budget authority (and thus some of the savings from the caps would occur beyond the 10-year budget window) and because some budget authority never results in outlays.

Program Integrity Initiatives

The Budget Control Act of 2011, as proposed on August 1, 2011, includes two program integrity initiatives aimed at reducing net federal spending for income security and health care programs. If funding is ultimately provided for those initiatives, their net budgetary effects would consist of an increase in discretionary spending to identify and reduce overpayments for such benefits, and some savings in the direct spending programs that provide those benefits (see Table 2).

The bill would allow adjustments to the discretionary caps that would permit additional appropriations to:

- The Social Security Administration (SSA) to conduct continuing disability reviews of beneficiaries of the Disability Insurance (DI) and Supplemental Security Income (SSI) programs and redeterminations (of the eligibility criteria other than disability) of SSI beneficiaries, and
- The Health Care Fraud and Abuse Control Account (HCFAC), which supports activities to reduce waste, fraud, and abuse in Medicare, Medicaid, and the Children's Health Insurance Program (CHIP).

The bill provides that the annual discretionary funding caps would be adjusted by the amounts appropriated for program integrity activities in excess of specific base amounts, up to specified maximum adjustments each year. Those base amounts, however, do not equal the amounts of spending for program integrity activities currently assumed in CBO's baseline. Accordingly, CBO's estimates of mandatory savings from program integrity activities are based on the differences between total funding under the bill (assuming the maximum possible cap adjustment) and the spending in CBO's baseline rather than the total amount of the cap adjustments.

For Congressional scorekeeping purposes, the benefit savings would not be counted as an offset to direct spending, pursuant to Congressional scorekeeping guidelines published in the conference report for the Balanced Budget Act of 1997 (P.L. 105-3 3). Specifically, Scorekeeping Rule 3 states that "entitlements and other mandatory programs... will be scored at current law levels unless Congressional action modifies the authorization legislation." In other words, even though additional discretionary funding for the administration of such programs might lead to budgetary savings (from reduced benefit payments), such savings are not counted as reductions in direct spending for scorekeeping purposes.

Social Security Administration

The annual discretionary funding caps would be adjusted by the amount by which funds appropriated for the SSA program integrity activities for a year exceed $273 million; the maximum such adjustment would rise from $623 million for fiscal year 2012 to $1.309 billion a year for fiscal years 2017 through 2021. If the Congress were to appropriate the maximum amounts eligible for the cap adjustment related to SSA funding, spending for such activities would be about $4 billion above CBO's baseline. Based on the $4 billion increase, CBO estimates that benefit outlays for DI, SSI, Medicare, and Medicaid would fall by nearly $12 billion over the 2012-202 1 period (see Table 2). Additional savings would accrue after 2021.

Health Care Fraud and Abuse Control

The discretionary caps would also be adjusted by the amount by which funds appropriated for HCFAC for a year exceed $311 million, subject to a maximum adjustment that would rise from $270 million for fiscal year 2012 to $496 million for fiscal year 2021. If the Congress were to appropriate the maximum amounts eligible for the cap adjustment related to HCFAC, spending for such activities would be about $3 billion above CBO's baseline. Based on that increase, CBO estimates that benefit outlays for Medicare, Medicaid, and CHIP would fall by about $3.7 billion over the 2012-2021 period. Additional savings would accrue after 2021.

Changes in Direct Spending for Education Programs

Title V of the Budget Control Act of 2011 would amend the Higher Education Act of 1965 to appropriate additional funds for the federal Pell Grant program and make two changes to the Federal Student Loan Program. CBO estimates that, on net, those changes would increase direct spending by $7.4 billion over the 2012-2016 period but reduce direct spending by $4.6 billion over the 2012-202 1 period (see Table 3).

Pell Grants

The bill would directly appropriate $10.0 billion for fiscal year 2012 and $7.0 billion for fiscal year 2013 for Pell grants. Those funds would be used to supplement funding for the portion of the Pell Grant program that is funded through annual discretionary appropriations. CBO estimates that this provision would increase direct spending by $17.0 billion over the 2012-2015 period (with no impact on outlays after 2015).

Student Loans

As required under the Federal Credit Reform Act of 1990, most of the costs of the federal student loan programs are estimated on a net-present-value basis.[2] The bill would make two changes to the student loan programs. CBO estimates those changes would reduce direct spending by $9.6 billion over the 2012-2016 period and $21.6 billion over the 2012-202 1 period. The legislation would:

- *Eliminate the subsidized loan program for graduate students.* Beginning July 1, 2012, the bill would eliminate the interest subsidy on subsidized student loans for almost all graduate students while a borrower is in school, in the post-school grace period, and during any authorized deferment period. (Certain post-baccalaureate students would still be eligible.) The current annual and cumulative loan limits for unsubsidized loans would be adjusted to permit students to borrow additional funds in the unsubsidized loan program. CBO projects that, over the 2012-202 1 period, the provision would shift approximately $125 billion in loan volume from the subsidized to the unsubsidized loan program. Because borrowers would be responsible for the interest accrued on those loans while in school, CBO estimates that this provision would reduce direct spending by $8.2 billion over the 20 12- 2016 period and $18.1 billion over the 2012-2021 period.
- *Eliminate loan repayment incentives.* Beginning July 1, 2012, the bill would terminate, with one exception, the Secretary of Education's authority to make incentive payments to borrowers to encourage the on-time repayment of their federal loans. Specifically, the bill would eliminate the Secretary's authority to offer a partial rebate of the origination fee but would still allow the current interest rate reduction for borrowers who agree to repay their loans through electronic debiting.[3]Because borrowers would effectively pay a higher upfront origination fee, CBO estimates this provision would reduce direct spending by $1.4 billion over the 2012-2016 period and $3.6 billion over the 2012-2021 period.

Other Provisions

The legislation would allow for staggered increases in the debt limit through a series of actions by the President, which could be overturned by enactment of joint resolutions of disapproval. If the President took all such actions, the debt limit would eventually be raised by at least $2.1 trillion; the increase could be as much as $2.4 trillion if certain Congressional actions occurred as well. In addition, the bill would establish procedures for enforcing the caps on discretionary spending and would provide for a vote on a balanced budget amendment by the end of December 2011.

The legislation also would establish a Congressional Joint Select Committee on Deficit Reduction charged with a goal of reducing the deficit by at least $1.5 trillion between 2012 and 2021. If, by January 15, 2012, enactment of legislation originating with the joint select committee does not achieve an estimated $1.2 trillion in deficit reduction (including an allowance for interest savings), the bill would require reductions in both discretionary and direct spending to make up for any shortfall in that targeted savings. Those automatic reductions in spending would be spread evenly over the fiscal years 2013 through 2021; half would come from defense spending and half from nondefense spending, including both discretionary and direct spending.

Those reductions would be implemented as follows:

- The reductions in discretionary spending in 2013 would be accomplished by cutting the budgetary resources available for defense and nondefense accounts by the respective percentages necessary to achieve the required reductions for that year. The reductions in discretionary spending in 2014 through 2021 would be accomplished by lowering the caps on discretionary budget authority for those years. For the purpose of lowering those caps, the bill would set separate caps on funding for defense and nondefense purposes.
- The reductions in direct spending would be implemented using the procedures specified in the Statutory Pay-As-You-Go (PAYGO) Act of 2010 (title I ofP.L. 111-139). Under that act, budgetary resources available for programs subject to the automatic reductions, with the exception of Medicare, would be cut by a uniform percentage sufficient to achieve the total required outlay savings for a year. Many direct spending programs and activities would be exempt, however, including Social Security and other retirement programs, Medicaid, and certain other programs benefiting low-income people. The legislation would limit Medicare cuts to no more than 2 percent.

OVERALL BUDGETARY IMPACT OF THE LEGISLATION

In total, if appropriations in the next 10 years are equal to the caps on discretionary spending and the maximum amount of funding is provided for the program integrity initiatives, CBO estimates that the legislation—apart from the provisions related to the joint select committee—would reduce budget deficits by $917 billion between 2012 and 2021. In addition, legislation originating with the joint select committee, or the automatic reductions in spending that would occur in the absence of such legislation, would reduce deficits by at least $1.2 trillion over the 10-year period. Therefore, the deficit reduction stemming from this legislation would total at least $2.1 trillion over the 2012-202 1 period (see Table 3). Those amounts are relative to CBO's March 2011 baseline adjusted for subsequent appropriation action.

Apart from the provisions related to the joint select committee, savings in discretionary spending would amount to $741 billion, mandatory spending would be reduced by $20 billion, and the savings in interest on the public debt because of the lower deficits would come to $156 billion. (CBO's cost estimates for legislation do not ordinarily include effects on debt service costs, but CBO provides such estimates, when requested, for broad budget plans.) The composition of the other $1.2 trillion in savings over time and across budget categories would depend on the specific provisions of any legislation stemming from proposals of the joint select committee and the extent of any automatic reductions that would be triggered.

CBO has also calculated the net budgetary impact if discretionary savings are measured relative to its January baseline projections. Relative to that baseline, CBO estimates that the legislation would reduce budget deficits by at least $2.3 trillion between 2012 and 2021. Apart from the provisions related to the joint select committee, savings in discretionary spending would amount to $920 billion, mandatory spending would be reduced by $20 billion, and the savings in interest on the public debt because of the lower deficits would come to $196 billion.

I hope this information is useful to you. If you wish further details on this analysis, we will be pleased to provide them.

Sincerely,

Douglas W. Elmendorf
Director

Attachments
cc: Honorable Nancy Pelosi House Democratic Leader
Honorable Mitch McConnell Senate Republican Leader

Table 1. Projected Savings from Discretionary Caps as Specified in the Budget Control Act of 2011, as Posted on the Web Site of the House Committee on Rules on August 1, 2011 (By fiscal year, in billions of dollars)

					Projections of Discretionary Spending							
		2012	2013	2014	2015	2016	2017	2018	2019	2020	2021	Total, 2012-2021
CBO's March 2011 Baseline	BA	1,266	1,290	1,318	1,346	1,377	1,413	1,450	1,488	1,526	1,565	14,038
	OT	1,344	1,356	1,371	1,391	1,420	1,446	1,475	1,517	1,556	1,594	14,472
Adjustments												
Exclude funding for operations in Afghanistan	BA	-161	-164	-167	-170	-173	-177	-180	-184	-188	-192	-1,756
and Iraq and for similar activities	OT	-76	-131	-153	-163	-169	-172	-175	-180	-184	-187	-1,589
Incorporate final 2011 appropriations	BA	-17	-17	-18	-18	-18	-18	-19	-19	-19	-20	-183
	OT	-2	-8	-11	-12	-13	-14	-15	-15	-16	-16	-122
Adjusted March 2011 Baseline	BA	1,087	1,109	1,134	1,159	1,186	1,218	1,251	1,285	1,319	1,353	12,099
	OT	1,267	1,217	1,207	1,216	1,238	1,260	1,285	1,323	1,357	1,391	12,760
CBO's January 2011 Baseline Excluding Funding for	BA	1,111	1,133	1,157	1,182	1,210	1,242	1,275	1,309	1,343	1,377	12,341
Operations in Afghanistan and Iraq and for Similar Activities	OT	1,275	1,230	1,224	1,233	1,257	1,280	1,306	1,344	1,378	1,412	12,939
						Proposal						
Proposed Discretionary Caps on	BA	1,043	1,047	1,066	1,086	1,107	1,131	1,156	1,182	1,208	1,234	11,260
Budget Authority[a]	OT	1,241	1,170	1,148	1,149	1,164	1,179	1,196	1,226	1,252	1,278	12,004
					Effect of Proposed Discretionary Caps							
Relative to the Adjusted March 2011 Baseline	BA	-44	-62	-68	-73	-79	-87	-95	-103	-111	-119	-840
	OT	-25	-47	-59	-67	-74	-81	- 89	-97	-104	-112	-756
Relative to the January 2011	BA	-68	-86	-92	-97	-103	-111	-119	-127	-135	-144	-1,081

		Projections of Discretionary Spending										
		2012	2013	2014	2015	2016	2017	2018	2019	2020	2021	Total, 2012-2021
Baseline Excluding Funding for												
Operations in Afghanistan and Iraq and for Similar Activities	OT	-33	-60	-76	-84	-93	-101	-110	-118	-126	-134	-935

SOURCE: Congressional Budget Office.

NOTES: The calculations above do not include any adjustments for program integrity initiatives.

BA = budget authority; OT = outlays.

[a]. CBO calculated outlays for 2012 to 2021 by assuming an average aggregate spendout rate for all discretionary spending.

Table 2. Estimated Effects of Program Integrity Initiatives in the Budget Control Act of 2011, as Posted on the Web Site of the House Committee on Rules on August 1, 2011 (By fiscal year, in millions of dollars)

	2012	2013	2014	2015	2016	2017	2018	2019	2020	2021	2012-2021
			Cap Adjustments in the Legislation (Subject to Appropriation)[a]								
SSA											
Budget Authority	623	751	924	1,123	1,166	1,309	1,309	1,309	1,309	1,309	11,130
Outlays	536	689	891	1,083	1,146	1,286	1,299	1,309	1,309	1,309	10,857
HCFAC											
Budget Authority	270	299	329	361	395	414	434	454	475	496	3,927
Outlays	238	296	325	357	391	412	432	452	472	493	3,867
Total											
Budget Authority	893	1,050	1,253	1,484	1,561	1,723	1,743	1,763	1,784	1,805	15,057
Outlays	774	985	1,216	1,440	1,537	1,698	1,731	1,761	1,781	1,802	14,724
			Non-Scorable Effects on Direct Spending Outlays								
SSA[b]	-47	-248	-464	-709	-1,033	-1,340	-1,627	-1,928	-2,147	-2,327	-11,872

Table 2. (Continued)

	2012	2013	2014	2015	2016	2017	2018	2019	2020	2021	2012 -2021
			Non-Scorable Effects on Direct Spending Outlays								
HCFAC	-84	-185	-290	-402	-435	-453	-467	-475	-476	-475	-3,741
Total	-132	-433	-754	-1,111	-1,468	-1,794	-2,094	-2,402	-2,623	-2,802	-15,614
Memorandum:											
Changes in Outlays for Program Integrity Activities above Baseline[c]											
SSA	95	179	306	456	474	566	529	487	433	375	3,900
HCFAC	225	267	281	297	314	317	318	317	316	314	2,967
Total	320	446	587	753	788	883	847	804	749	689	6,867

SOURCE: Congressional Budget Office.

NOTE: SSA = Social Security Administration; HCFAC = Health Care Fraud and Abuse Control Account.

[a]. These amounts reflect the cap adjustments (budget authority) specified in the legislation. Because the base level of budget authority for program integrity activities specified in the bill (that is, the level of funding that is necessary to trigger a cap adjustment) is lower than the amount assumed in CBO's baseline, only part of the cap adjustment reflects potential new spending for program integrity activities over and above the amounts projected in CBO's baseline.

[b]. The legislation does not allocate the proposed spending increases among the different activities. CBO assumed spending would be allocated in the same proportions as under the President's budget request. In that case, the spending proposed in this legislation would not exceed baseline spending for SSI redeterminations in any year or for SSI continuing disability reviews in fiscal years 2020 or 2021.

[c]. Increased spending above CBO's baseline assuming the appropriation of the maximum cap adjustment. CBO used those amounts to estimate the mandatory program savings.

Table 3. Effect on the Deficit of the Budget Control Act of 2011, as Posted on the Web Site of the House Committee on Rules on August 1, 2011, Relative to CBO's March 2011 Baseline, Adjusted to Reflect Enactment of 2011 (By fiscal year, in billions of dollars)

	2012	2013	2014	2015	2016	2017	2018	2019	2020	2021	Total 2012-2021
Discretionary Spending Establishment of caps	-25	-47	-59	-67	-74	-81	-89	-97	-104	-112	-756
Program integrity[a]	1	1	1	1	2	2	2	2	2	2	15
Subtotal	-25	-46	-58	-66	-73	-79	-87	-95	-103	-111	-741
Mandatory Spending[b] Program integrity	0	0	-1	-1	-1	-2	-2	-2	-3	-3	-16
Pell grants	4	8	5	0	0	0	0	0	0	0	17
Other education	-1	-2	-2	-2	-2	-2	-2	-2	-2	-3	-22
Subtotal	3	5	2	-3	-4	-4	-4	-5	-5	-5	-20
Debt Service	0	-1	-3	-6	-10	-15	-20	-26	-33	-40	-156
Total Effect on the Deficit Excluding											
Provisions Related to the Joint Select											
Committee on Deficit Reduction[c]	-21	-42	-59	-75	-87	-99	-112	-126	-141	-156	-917
Provisions Related to the Joint Select											

Table 3. (Continued)

	2012	2013	2014	2015	2016	2017	2018	2019	2020	2021	Total 2012-2021
Committee on Deficit Reduction[c]	d	d	d	d	d	d	d	d	d	d	-1,200
Total Effect on the Deficit[c]	d	d	d	d	d	d	d	d	d	d	-2,117

Source: Congressional Budget Office.

Notes: The only budgetary effects in this table that are counted as changes in direct spending for Congressional scorekeeping purposes are the estimated changes in spending for Pell Grants and other education programs. With the effects of the discretionary caps measured relative to CBO's January baseline, the legislation, apart from the provisions related to the joint select committee, would reduce budget deficits by about $1.1 trillion between 2012 and 2021. Savings in discretionary spending would amount to $920 billion, mandatory spending would be reduced by $20 billion, and the savings in interest on the public debt because of the lower deficits would come to $196 billion. Including the provisions related to the joint select committee, the legislation would reduce budget deficits by at least $2.3 trillion relative to CBO's January baseline.

[a]. These amounts reflect the cap adjustments (budget authority) specified in the legislation. Because the base level of budget authority for program activities specified in the bill (that is, the level of funding that is necessary to trigger a cap adjustment) is lower than the amount assumed in CBO's baseline, only part of the cap adjustment reflects potential new spending for program integrity activities over and above the amounts projected in CBO's baseline. The amounts of potential new spending above baseline are shown in Table 2.

[b]. In addition, the Joint Select Committee on Deficit Reduction could spend existing funds upon startup near the end of fiscal year 2011; CBO estimates that would constitute an increase in direct spending of less than $500,000 in 2011.

[c]. Negative numbers indicate a reduction in the deficit.

[d]. The composition of the other $1.2 trillion in savings over time and across budget categories would depend on the specific provisions of any legislation stemming from proposals of the joint select committee and the extent of any automatic reductions that would be triggered.

End Notes

[1]. For purposes of the discretionary caps, the security category comprises discretionary appropriations for the Department of Defense, the Department of Homeland Security, the Department of Veterans Affairs, the National Nuclear Security Administration, the intelligence community management account (95-0401-0-1-054), and all budget accounts in budget function 150 (international affairs). The nonsecurity category comprises all discretionary appropriations not included in the security category.

[2]. Under credit reform, the present value of all loan-related cash flows is calculated by discounting those expected cash flows to the year of disbursement, using the rates for comparable maturities on U.S. Treasury borrowing. (For example, the cash flow for a two-year loan is discounted using the Treasury rate for a two-year zero-coupon note.)

[3]. Under current law for the partial rebate, borrowers initially pay only 0.5 percent of the 1-percent borrower origination fee on subsidized and unsubsidized loans. If a borrower makes 12 on-time payments in the first year of repayment, the Secretary will forgive the additional 0.5 percent of the origination fee. In addition, parent and GradPLUS borrowers initially pay only 2.5 percent of their 4-percent borrower origination fee. Borrowers who make 12 on-time payments in the first year are forgiven the additional 1.5 percent of the origination fee.

In: The Budget Control Act of 2011
Editors: C. G. Lynch and C. McHale ISBN: 978-1-61942-035-9

Chapter 3

THE DEBT LIMIT: HISTORY AND RECENT INCREASES*

D. Andrew Austin and Mindy R. Levit

SUMMARY

Total federal debt can increase in two ways. First, debt increases when the government sells debt to the public to finance budget deficits and acquire the financial resources needed to meet its obligations. This increases *debt held by the public*. Second, debt increases when the federal government issues debt to certain government accounts, such as the Social Security, Medicare, and Transportation trust funds, in exchange for their reported surpluses. This increases *debt held by government accounts*. The sum of *debt held by the public* and *debt held by government accounts* is the total federal debt. Surpluses reduce debt held by the public, while deficits raise it. Treasury Secretary Timothy Geithner announced that the federal debt reached its statutory limit on May 16, 2011 and declared a debt issuance suspension period, allowing certain extraordinary measures to extend Treasury's borrowing capacity until early August 2011. Since May 16, debt subject to limit has hovered just below $14,294 billion. On August 2, 2011, President Obama signed into law the Budget Control Act of 2011 (S. 365), which included numerous provisions aimed at deficit reduction and an increase in the debt limit of up to $2,400 billion that would occur in several stages.

---

* This is an edited, reformatted and augmented version of a Congressional Research Service publication, CRS Report for Congress RL31967, from www.crs.gov, dated August 3, 2011.

Congress has always placed restrictions on federal debt. The form of debt restrictions, structured as amendments to the Second Liberty Bond Act of 1917, evolved into a general debt limit in 1939. Congress has voted to raise the debt limit 10 times since 2001, due to persistent deficits and additions to federal trust funds. Congress raised the limit in June 2002, and by December 2002 the U.S. Treasury asked Congress for another increase, which passed in May 2003. In June 2004, the U.S. Treasury asked for another debt limit increase. After Congress recessed in mid-October 2004 without acting, the Treasury Secretary told Congress he could keep debt below its limit only through mid-November. A debt limit increase was enacted on November 19, 2004. In 2005, reconciliation instructions in the FY2006 budget resolution (H.Con.Res. 95) included a debt limit increase. After warnings from the U.S. Treasury, Congress passed an increase that the President signed on March 20. In 2007, Congress approved legislation (H.J.Res. 43) to raise the debt limit by $850 billion to $9,815 billion that the President signed September 29, 2007.

The recent economic slowdown led to sharply higher deficits in recent years, which led to a series of debt limit increases. The Housing and Economic Recovery Act of 2008 (H.R. 3221), signed into law (P.L. 110-289) on July 30, 2008, included a debt limit increase. The Emergency Economic Stabilization Act of 2008 (H.R. 1424), signed into law on October 3 (P.L. 110-343), raised the debt limit again. The debt limit rose a third time in less than a year to $12,104 billion with the passage of the American Recovery and Reinvestment Act of 2009 on February 13, 2009 (ARRA; H.R. 1), which was signed into law on February 17, 2009 (P.L. 111-5).

Following this measure, the debt limit was subsequently increased by $290 billion to $12,394 billion (P.L. 111-123) in a stand-alone debt limit bill on December 28, 2009, and by $1.9 trillion to $14,294 billion on February 12, 2010 (P.L. 111-139) as part of a package that also contained the Statutory Pay-As-You-Go Act of 2010. Following enactment of the Budget Control Act of 2011 (P.L. 112-25) and the submission of a certification letter from President Obama to the Congress, the debt limit was increased on August 2, 2011, by $400 billion, to $14,694 billion.

INTRODUCTION

The statutory debt limit applies to almost all federal debt.[1] The limit applies to federal debt held by the public (that is, debt held outside the federal government itself) and to federal debt held by the government's own accounts. Federal trust funds, such as Social Security, Medicare, Transportation, and

Civil Service Retirement accounts, hold most of this internally held debt.[2] The government's surpluses or deficits determine essentially all of the change in debt held by the public.[3] The government's on-budget fiscal balance, which excludes a small U.S. Postal Service net surplus or deficit and a large Social Security surplus of payroll taxes net of paid benefits, does not directly affect debt held in government accounts.[4] Increases or decreases in debt held by government accounts result from net financial flows into accounts holding the debt, such as the Social Security Trust Fund. Legal requirements and government accounting practices also affect levels of debt held by government accounts.[5]

Slowing the growth in federal debt by cutting spending has been suggested by some commentators as a means of avoiding an increase in the debt limit. The scale of spending reductions that would be required, as of late spring 2011, would likely have approximately equaled total discretionary spending for the last five months of FY2011. FY2011 ends on September 30, 2011.[6]

Recent Legislative Initiatives

A bill (H.R. 1954) to raise the debt limit to $16,700 billion was introduced on May 24 and was defeated in a May 31, 2011, House vote of 97 to 318. The House passed the Cut, Cap, and Balance Act of 2011 (H.R. 2560; 234-190 vote) on July 19, 2011. On July 22, the Senate tabled the bill on a 51-46 vote. The measure would have increased the statutory limit on federal debt from $14,294 billion to $16,700 billion once a proposal for a constitutional amendment requiring a balanced federal budget was transmitted to the states.

On August 2, 2011, President Obama signed into law the Budget Control Act of 2011 (P.L. 112- 25), following House approval of the measure by a vote of 269-161 on August 1, 2011, and Senate approval by a vote of 74-26 on August 2, 2011.[7] Included in this measure were numerous provisions aimed at deficit reduction and an increase in the debt limit of up to $2,400 billion ($2.4 trillion) that would occur in several stages. Included in this measure are major provisions that

- impose discretionary spending caps, enforced by automatic spending reductions, referred to as a sequester;[8]
- establish a Joint Select Committee on Deficit Reduction, whose recommendations would be eligible for expedited consideration;

- require a vote on a joint resolution on a proposed constitutional amendment to mandate a balanced federal budget;[9] and
- institute a mechanism allowing for the President and Treasury Secretary to raise the debt ceiling, subject to congressional disapproval.

The legislation provides a three-step procedure by which the debt limit can be increased. First, the debt limit was raised by $400 billion, to $14,694 billion on August 2, 2011, following a letter to Congress from President Obama certifying that the debt was within $100 billion of the legal limit.[10] Second, the debt limit will be further increased by $500 billion within 50 days of the certification, pending the consideration of a joint resolution of disapproval, which would be subject to a presidential veto. If the joint resolution is not enacted, the second tier increase in the debt limit will occur. Following these increases, the debt limit can be further increased by up to $1.5 trillion.[11] This step in the process would allow for a debt limit increase of $1.5 trillion if the states have received a balanced budget amendment for ratification. Otherwise, the debt limit could be increased by between $1.2 trillion and $1.5 trillion depending on the level of deficit reduction enacted as a result of the recommendations of the Joint Select Committee on Deficit Reduction. If neither of these apply, then the debt limit would be increased by $1.2 trillion.

THE DEBT LIMIT AND THE TREASURY

Standard methods of financing federal activities or meeting government obligations used by the U.S. Department of Treasury (Treasury) can be hobbled when federal debt nears its legal limit. The government's income and outlays vary over the course of the year, producing monthly surpluses and deficits that affect the level of debt, whether or not the government has a surplus or deficit for the entire year. Even major government trust fund accounts that usually run annual surpluses can swing back and forth between deficits and surpluses on a month-to-month basis.

The ability to borrow is central to Treasury cash management systems that handle fluctuations in federal revenues and outlays. When federal debt has neared the debt limit in the past, limiting the U.S. Treasury's borrowing authority, financial management has become more complicated.

If the U.S. Treasury were precluded from borrowing due to a binding debt limit in times when federal outlays outpaced revenues, the government would no longer meet all of its legal obligations in a timely manner.[12] If the limit prevents the Treasury from issuing new debt to manage short-term cash flows or to finance an annual deficit, the government may be unable to obtain the cash needed to pay its bills or it may be unable to invest the surpluses of designated government accounts (federal trust funds) in federal debt as generally required by law. In either case, the Treasury is left in a bind; the law requires that the government's legal obligations be paid, but the debt limit may prevent it from issuing the debt that would allow it to do so on time.

Among other consequences, a sustained inability to pay obligations on time could hinder the U.S. Treasury's ability to borrow on advantageous terms in the future. The Government Accountability Office has also concluded that delays in debt limit increases could lead to "serious negative consequences for the Treasury market and increase borrowing costs."[13] A delay in interest payments on Treasury securities would trigger a default and risk serious negative repercussions for economies and financial markets around the world. Default might be avoided in such situations by delaying other types of federal payments and transfers. A government that delays payment of an obligation, in effect, borrows from vendors, contractors, beneficiaries, state and local governments, or employees who are not paid on time. In some cases, delaying payments incurs interest penalties under some statutes such as the Prompt Payment Act, which directs the government to pay interest penalties to contractors if it does not pay them by the required payment date,[14] and the Internal Revenue Code, which requires the government to pay interest penalties if tax refunds are delayed beyond a certain date.[15]

Several credit ratings agencies and investment banks have expressed concerns about the consequences to the financial system and the economy if the U.S. Treasury were unable to fund federal obligations.[16] Many economists and financial institutions have stated that if the market associated Treasury securities with default risks, the effects on global capital markets could be significant.[17]

Past Treasury Secretaries, when faced with a nearly binding debt ceiling, have used special strategies to handle cash and debt management responsibilities. Actions taken in the past include suspending sales of nonmarketable debt, postponing or downsizing marketable debt auctions, and withholding receipts that would be transferred to certain government trust funds. Congress has authorized the Treasury Secretary to invoke a "debt issuance suspension period" to use some of these strategies using the Civil

Service Retirement Fund and the Thrift Savings Fund, along with the authority to make those funds whole after an easing of the debt constraint.[18]

Some U.S. Treasury responses to the credit crunch that began in mid-2007 created balance sheet items that have expanded options available to the Treasury Secretary, although such options would have minor effects on delaying when federal debt would reach its legal limit. The U.S. Treasury began selling off certain mortgage-backed securities (MBSs) acquired in late 2008.[19] The pace of those sales was targeted at $10 billion per month in order to minimize any market disruptions in the mortgage securities market, and thus is unlikely to affect the timing of when the U.S. Treasury will reach the debt limit significantly. By the end of April 2011, the U.S. Treasury had sold $121 billion of its $225 billion portfolio of MBSs.[20] Even with proceeds of these or other potential asset sales however, the U.S. Treasury is unlikely to maintain smooth debt management operations indefinitely in the face of a continuing imbalance between federal revenues and outlays without an increase in the debt limit. U.S. Treasury contends that other types of asset sales are unlikely to provide a prudent or practical method of easing debt limit constraints.[21]

Why Have a Debt Limit?

The debt limit can hinder the Treasury's ability to manage the federal government's finances, as noted above. In extreme cases, when the federal debt is very near its statutory limit, the Treasury must take unusual and extraordinary measures to meet federal obligations.[22] While the debt limit has never caused the federal government to default on its obligations, it has at times caused great inconvenience and has added uncertainty to Treasury operations.

The debt limit also provides Congress with the strings to control the federal purse, allowing Congress to assert its constitutional prerogatives to control spending.[23] The debt limit also imposes a form of fiscal accountability that compels Congress and the President to take visible action to allow further federal borrowing when the federal government spends more than it collects in revenues. In the words of one author, the debt limit "expresses a national devotion to the idea of thrift and to economical management of the fiscal affairs of the government."[24] On the other hand, some budget experts have advocated elimination of the debt limit, arguing that other controls provided by the modern congressional budget process established in 1974 have superseded the debt limit, and that the limit does little to alter spending and revenue policies that determine the size of the federal deficit.[25]

A Brief History of the Federal Debt Limit

Origins of the Federal Debt Limit

Congress has always placed restrictions on federal debt. Limitations on federal debt have helped Congress assert its constitutional powers of the purse, of taxation, and the initiation of war. Between World War I and World War II the form of statutory restrictions on federal debt evolved into an aggregate limit that applied to nearly all federal debt outstanding.

Before World War I, Congress often authorized borrowing for specified purposes, such as the construction of the Panama Canal.[26] Congress also often specified which types of financial instruments Treasury could employ, and specified or limited interest rates, maturities, and details of when bonds could be redeemed. In other cases, especially in time of war, Congress provided the Treasury with discretion, subject to broad limits, to choose debt instruments.[27] Some opponents raised concerns that granting the Treasury Secretary authority to issue debt could affect monetary policies, which might tighten credit conditions. Proponents contended that federal borrowing would not disrupt settlements on such monetary issues reached in 1878 and 1890.

Such concerns became moot after the establishment of the Federal Reserve System in 1913.

For example, the War Revenue Act of 1898 allowed Treasury to use certificates of indebtedness, which had maturities of a year or less, and were used for short-term borrowing and cash management, as well as long-term bonds.[28] For example, the 1898 War Revenue Act (30 Stat. 448-470) that funded Spanish-American War costs granted the Treasury Secretary the authority to have $100 million outstanding in certificates of indebtedness with maturities under a year, which were mainly sold to large investors, banks, and other financial institutions. The act also allowed the Treasury to issue $400 million in longer-term notes and bonds, which were made available to public subscription, allowing smaller investors to participate. Proponents of the act, however, made clear their intention to allow the Treasury Secretary substantial administrative leeway within those limits.[29]

Over time, the leeway granted the Treasury Secretary tended to expand. For example, the Second Liberty Bond Act of 1917, which helped finance the

United States' entry into World War I, dropped certain limits on the maturity and redemption of bonds.[30] The act also incorporated unused borrowing capacity authorized by the First Liberty Bond Act (40 Stat 35; P.L. 65-3) and other previous borrowing acts.[31] Separate limits for previous debt issues, however, were retained in the text of that act—an overall aggregated debt limit evolved later. Features of debt authorized by previous acts, such as the broad tax exemption for First Liberty Bond Act securities, remained intact.

Subsequent borrowing measures were drafted as amendments to Second Liberty Bond Act until 1982.[32] Setting debt policy by amendments to the Second Liberty Bond Act of 1917 rather than through original statutes reflected changes in legislative drafting practices at that time.[33]

In the 1920s, Congress provided Treasury Secretary Andrew Mellon with additional leeway in order to replace expensive older federal debt with cheaper new issues. Congress allowed Treasury to issue notes, a financial instrument issued extensively in the Civil War and rarely thereafter, and limited the amount of notes outstanding, rather than the sum of issuances, which gave greater Treasury flexibility to roll over debt. Savings certificates designed for small investors were also reintroduced.[34]

In the 1930s, Congress moved towards aggregate constraints on federal borrowing that allowed the Treasury greater ability to respond to changing conditions and more flexibility in financial management. In March 1939, President Franklin Roosevelt and Treasury Secretary Henry Morgenthau asked Congress to eliminated separate limits on bonds and on other types of debt.[35]

The House approved the measure (H.R. 5748) on March 23, 1939, the Senate passed it on June 1 (P.L. 76-201). When enacted on June 20, the measure created the first aggregate limit ($45 billion) covering nearly all public debt.[36] Combining a $30 billion limit on bonds with a $15 billion limit on shorter-term debt, while retaining the $45 billion total limit in effect, enabled Treasury to roll over maturing notes into longer-term bonds. This measure gave the Treasury freer rein to manage the federal debt as it saw fit. Thus, the Treasury could issue debt instruments with maturities that would reduce interest costs and minimize financial risks stemming from future interest rate changes.[37] While a separate $4 billion limit for "National Defense" series securities was introduced in 1940, legislation in 1941 folded that borrowing authority back under an increased aggregate limit of $65 billion.[38]

Although the Treasury was delegated greater independence of action on the eve of the United States' entry into World War II, the debt limit at the time was much closer to total federal debt than it had been at the end of World War

I. For example, the 1919 Victory Liberty Bond Act (P.L. 65-328) raised the maximum allowable federal debt to $43 billion, far above the $25.5 billion in total federal debt at the end of FY1919.[39] By contrast, the debt limit in 1939 was $45 billion, only about 10% above the $40.4 billion total federal debt of that time.[40]

World War II and after

The debt ceiling was raised to accommodate accumulating costs for World War II in each year from 1941 through 1945, when it was set at $300 billion.[41] After World War II ended, the debt limit was reduced to $275 billion. Because the Korean War was mostly financed by higher taxes rather than by increased debt, the limit remained at $275 billion until 1954. After 1954, the debt limit was reduced twice and increased seven times, until March 1962 when it again reached $300 billion, its level at the end of World War II. Since March 1962, Congress has enacted 75 separate measures that have altered the limit on federal debt.[42] Most of these changes in the debt limit were, measured in percentage terms, small in comparison to changes adopted in wartime or during the Great Depression. Some recent increases in the debt limit, however, were large in dollar terms. For instance, in May 2003, the debt limit increased by $984 billion and in February 2010 the debt limit was increased by $1.9 trillion (P.L. 111-139).

THE DEBT CEILING IN THE LAST DECADE

During the four years (FY1998-FY2001) the government ran surpluses, federal debt held by intergovernmental accounts grew by $855 billion and debt held by the public fell by almost $450 billion. Since FY2001, however, debt held by the public has grown due to persistent and substantial budget deficits. Debt held in government accounts also has grown, in large part because Social Security payroll taxes have exceeded payments of beneficiaries. *Table 1* shows components of debt in current dollars and as percentages of gross domestic product (GDP).[43]

Figure 1 shows the components of federal debt as shares of gross domestic product (GDP) from FY1940 through FY2010.[44] Federal debt held by government accounts has grown steadily since 1980.

Table 1. Components of Debt Subject to Limit, FY1996-FY2010 (in billions of current dollars and as percentage of GDP)

		Total		Held by Government Accounts		Held by the Public	
End of Fiscal Year	Debt Limit	$ Billion	% of GDP	$ Billion	% of GDP	$ Billion	% of GDP
1996	$5,500	$5,137.2	65.7%	1,432.4	18.3%	3,704.8	47.4%
1997	5,950	5,327.6	64.2	1,581.9	19.0	3,745.8	45.1
1998	5,950	5,439.4	62.2	1,742.1	19.9	3,697.4	42.3
1999	5,950	5,567.7	60.1	1,958.2	21.1	3,609.5	38.9
2000	5,950	5,591.6	57.0	2,203.9	22.4	3,387.7	34.5
2001	5,950	5,732.8	56.6	2,436.5	24.1	3,296.3	32.5
2002	6,400	6,161.4	58.9	2,644.2	25.3	3,517.2	33.6
2003	7,384	6,737.6	61.4	2,846.7	25.9	3,890.8	35.5
2004	7,384	7,333.4	62.5	3,056.6	26.0	4,276.8	36.4
2005	8,184	7,871.0	64.0	3,301.0	26.9	4,570.1	37.2
2006	8,965	8,420.3	64.2	3,610.4	27.5	4,809.8	36.7
2007	9,815[a]	8,921.3	65.4	3,903.7	28.6	5,017.6	36.8
2008	10,615[b]	9,960.0	70.0	4,180.0	29.4	5,780.3	40.6
2009	12,104[c]	11,909.8	84.1	4,358.0	30.8	7,551.9	53.3
2010	14,294[d]	13,510.8	92.1	4,585.7	31.3	9,022.8	61.5
Change during FY1998 - FY2001		$405.2		$854.6		$-449.5	
Change during FY2002 - FY2010		$7,778.0		$2,073.1		$5,704.9	

Source: U.S. Department of the Treasury, Financial Management Service, Treasury Bulletin, June 2001 and December 2006. Bureau of the Public Debt, Monthly Statement of Public Debt, various issues. CRS calculations.

Notes: For the fiscal years 1996 through 2000, the amounts held by government accounts and held by the public are approximations. In 2001, the Treasury publications began distinguishing holders of debt subject to limit. The numbers in the table showing this breakdown for FY1996 through FY2000 were calculated by subtracting debts of the Federal Financing Bank, an arm of the Treasury whose debt is not subject to limit, from total debt held by government accounts. This calculation approximates the amount of that debt subject to limit. This approximation overestimates debt by billions of dollars because estimates of unamortized discount are unavailable. This adjusted amount was then subtracted from total debt subject to limit to produce an approximate measure of debt held by the public subject to limit. Because the amount held by government accounts is overestimated, the resulting measure of debt held by the public subject to limit is underestimated. Totals may not sum due to rounding.

[a] Debt limit increased September 29, 2007, to $9,815 billion.

[b] The debt limit was increased twice in 2008—to $10,615 billion on July 30 and then to $11,315 billion on October 3, at the start of FY2009.
[c] Debt limit was increased February 17, 2009, to $12,104 billion.
[d] Debt limit was increased February 12, 2010, to $14,294 billion.

Debt held by the public, which changes in response to total surpluses or deficits, grew as a share of GDP through the mid-1990s. After FY1992, deficits shrank, and from FY1998 through FY2001 the federal government ran surpluses.[45] Those surpluses, along with rapid GDP growth, reduced debt held by the public as a percentage of GDP. When large deficits returned and GDP growth slowed in the early 2000s, debt held by the public as a share of GDP again increased.

Smaller deficits in FY2006 and FY2007 led to smaller increases in publicly held debt. The total FY2007 deficit fell to 1.2% of GDP according to CBO.[46] Financial turmoil in 2007 and 2008 and a subsequent recession that began in late 2007 led to federal actions taken to stabilize the housing and financial markets. The recession reduced federal revenues and increased federal spending, leading to large deficits and a series of debt limit increases.

The Debt Limit Issue in 2002

Accumulating debt in government accounts produced most of the pressure on the debt limit that occurred early in 2002. As deficits reemerged in FY2002, increases in debt held by the public added to the pressure on the debt limit in the spring of 2002. During the four fiscal years with surpluses (FY1998-FY2001), the increases in federally held debt and decreases in debt held by the public produced a net increase of $405 billion in total debt subject to limit. At the beginning of FY2002 (October 1, 2001), debt subject to limit was within $217 billion of the existing $5,950 billion debt limit.[47] Between then and the end of May 2002, debt subject to limit increased by another $217 billion, divided between a $117 billion increase in debt held by government accounts and a $100 billion increase in debt held by the public, putting the debt close to the $5,950 billion limit. *Table A-1*, presented in the *Appendix A*, shows month-by-month debt totals and accumulations from September 2001 through December 2010.

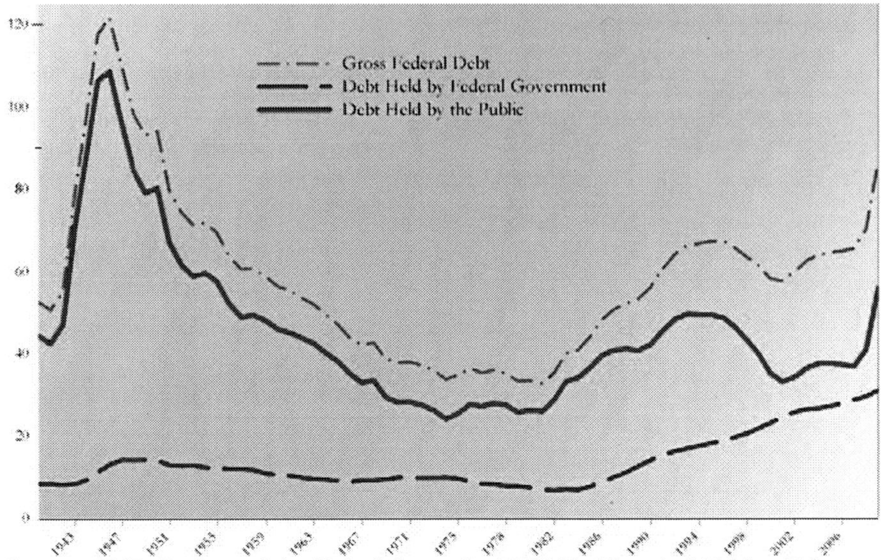

Source: OMB, Budget of the United States for FY2010, Historical Tables, February 2009; Mid-Session Review, August 2009.

Figure 1. Components of Federal Debt As a Percentage of GDP, FY1940-FY2009.

In the fall of 2001, the Administration recognized that a deteriorating budget outlook and continued growth in debt held by government accounts were likely to lead to the debt limit soon being reached. In early December 2001, it asked Congress to raise the debt limit by $750 billion to $6,700 billion. As the debt moved closer to and reached the debt limit over the first six months of FY2002, the Administration asked Congress repeatedly to increase the debt limit, warning of adverse financial consequences were the limit not raised.

On April 4, 2002, the Treasury held debt below the limit by invoking its legislatively mandated authority to suspend reinvestment of government securities in the G-Fund of the federal employees' Thrift Savings Plan (TSP). This allowed the Treasury to issue new debt and meet the government's obligations. On April 15, debt subject to limit stood at $5,949,975 million, just $25 million below the limit. Once April 15 tax revenues flowed in, the Treasury "made whole" the G-Fund by restoring all of the debt that had not been issued to the TSP over this period and crediting the fund with interest it would have earned on that debt.[48] By the end of April, debt subject to limit had fallen back $35 billion below the limit.

Resolving the Debt Limit Issue in 2002

By the middle of May 2002, debt subject to limit had again risen to within $15 million of the statutory limit. At the FY2002 average spending rate, $15 million equaled about five minutes of federal outlays. The Treasury, for the second time in 2002, used its statutory authority to avoid a default. The Treasury's financing problems, however, would persist without an increase in the debt limit. On May 14, the Treasury asked Congress to raise the debt limit or enact other statutory changes allowing the Treasury to issue new debt. A Treasury news release stated "absent extraordinary actions, the government will exceed the statutory debt ceiling no later than May 16," and that

> a "debt issuance suspension period" will begin no later than May 16 [2002].... [This] allows the Treasury to suspend or redeem investments in two trust funds, which will provide flexibility to fund the operations of the government during this period.[49]

The Treasury reduced federal debt held by these government accounts by replacing it with noninterest-bearing, non-debt instruments, which enabled it to issue new debt to meet the government's obligations. The Treasury claimed these extraordinary actions would suffice, at the latest, through June 28, 2002. Without a debt limit increase by that date, the Treasury indicated it would need to take other actions to avoid breaching the ceiling. By June 21, the Treasury had postponed a regular securities auction, but took no other actions. With large payments and other obligations due at the end of June and at the beginning of July, the Treasury stated it would soon exhaust all options to issue debt and fulfill government obligations, putting the government on the verge of a default.

During May and June 2002, Congress took steps to increase the debt limit. The FY2002 supplemental appropriations bill (H.R. 4775) passed by the House on May 24 included, after extended debate, language allowing any eventual House-Senate conference on the legislation to increase the debt limit. However, the Senate's supplemental appropriations bill (S. 2551; incorporated as an amendment to H.R. 4775, June 3, 2002) omitted debt-limit-increasing language. The Senate leadership expressed strong reluctance to include a debt limit increase in the supplemental appropriation bill. Instead, on June 11, the Senate adopted a bill (S. 2578), without debate, to raise the debt limit by $450 billion to $6,400 billion. At that time, a $450 billion debt limit increase was thought to provide enough borrowing authority for government operations through the rest of calendar year 2002, if not through the summer of 2003.

With the possibility of default looming over it, the House passed the $450 billion debt limit increase by a single vote on June 27. The President signed the bill into law on June 28 (P.L. 107-199, 116 Stat. 734), ending the 2002 debt limit crisis.[50]

The Debt Limit Issue in 2003

On Christmas Eve, 2002, Kenneth Dam, Deputy Secretary of the Treasury, sent a letter to Congress requesting an unspecified increase in the debt limit by late February 2003, signaling that the $6,400 billion debt limit would then be reached.[51] The 108th Congress, still in the process of organizing itself, did not immediately respond. Through the winter and into the spring, the Treasury repeatedly requested that the debt limit be raised to avoid serious financial problems. By February 20, 2003, the Treasury, as in 2002, used legislatively mandated measures to manage debt holdings of certain government accounts to avoid reaching the debt limit. These actions included the replacement of internally held government debt with non-debt instruments in certain government accounts and not issuing new debt to these accounts. These actions allowed the Treasury to issue additional debt to the public to acquire the cash needed to pay for the government's commitments or to issue new debt to other federal accounts.

Through the rest of February and into May, the Treasury held debt subject to limit $15 million below the debt ceiling.[52] The adoption of the conference report on the FY2004 budget resolution (H.Con.Res. 95; H.Rept. 108-71) on April 11, 2003, in the House triggered the "Gephardt rule" (House Rule XXVII) that deems to have passed legislation (in this case, H.J.Res. 51) raising the debt limit to accommodate the spending and revenue levels approved in the adopted budget resolution.[53]

The Senate received the debt-limit legislation on April 11, but did not act until May 23, after receiving further Treasury warnings of imminent default. On that day, debt subject to limit was $25 million (or 0.0004%) below the existing $6,400 billion limit. The Senate adopted the legislation, after rejecting eight amendments and sent it to the President, who signed it on May 27. This legislation raised the debt limit to $7,384 billion (P.L. 108-24, 117 Stat. 710).

The Debt Limit Issue in 2004

In January 2004, CBO estimated that the debt limit, then set at $7,384 billion, would be reached the following summer.[54] In June 2004, the Treasury asked Congress to raise the debt limit in order to avoid the disruptions to government finances experienced in the previous two years.[55] In August, and again in September, the Treasury declared that the debt limit would be reached in the first half of October. On October 14, debt subject to limit reached $7,383,975 million, just $25 million below the existing limit. The Treasury employed methods used in the previous two years to keep debt under the legal limit. On October 14, Secretary of the Treasury John Snow informed Congress, just before the election recess, that available measures to avoid breaching the debt limit would be exhausted by mid-November.[56] Without an increase in the debt limit, the Treasury would be unable to meet all of the government's existing obligations, which could undermine the U.S. government's reputation in capital markets and raise costs of federal borrowing.

Although the House passed a budget resolution for FY2005 in the spring of 2004, it did not reach final agreement with the Senate on the measure. Without a budget resolution passed by Congress, no resolution to raise the debt limit could be deemed passed by the House automatically under the Gephardt rule. Consequently, no measure was available to send to the Senate. As the debt approached the limit through the summer and into the fall, no legislation was moved to raise the debt limit.

Earlier, in September 2004, the House had added an amendment to the FY2005 Transportation-Treasury appropriations (H.R. 5025) in an effort to remove the Treasury's flexibility in financing the government as federal debt approached and reached the existing limit. Without that flexibility, the government would be unable to meet its financial obligations as the amount of debt neared the limit. The legislation cleared the House, but the Senate did not act on it.

After the elections, Senator Frist, on November 16, 2004, introduced legislation (S. 2986) to raise the debt limit by $800 billion, from $7,384 billion to $8,184 billion. The Senate approved the increase on November 17, 2004. The House considered and approved the increase on November 18. The President signed the legislation into law (P.L. 108-415, 118 Stat. 2337) on November 19, 2004. Estimates made at that time anticipated the new limit would be reached between August and December 2005.

Shortly before the increase in the debt limit, the Treasury delayed a debt auction and informed Congress that it would invoke a "debt limit suspension period" as it had in previous years. The increase in the debt limit in mid-November allowed the Treasury to reschedule the debt auction and cancel, before it began, the "debt limit suspension period."

The Debt Limit Issue in 2005, 2006, and 2007

Debt limit increases in 2005, 2006, and 2007 took a less dramatic path than those in President Bush's first term. In 2005, Congress included three reconciliation instructions in the FY2006 budget resolution (H.Con.Res. 95, 109th Congress; April 28, 2005), the third of which directed the House Committee on Ways and Means and the Senate Finance Committee to report bills raising the debt limit. The instructions specified a $781 billion debt limit increase, to $8,965 billion, with a reporting date of no later than September 30, 2005. Neither committee reported a bill to raise the debt limit.

The adoption of the conference report on the FY2006 budget resolution in late April 2005 also triggered the Gephardt rule (House Rule XXVII), producing a House Joint Resolution (H.J.Res. 47) that also would raise the debt limit by $781 billion to $8,965 billion. Under the rule, the resolution was automatically deemed passed by the House and sent to the Senate. Through the end of the first session of the 109th Congress, the Senate had not considered H.J.Res. 47, nor had Congress considered a reconciliation bill raising the debt limit as called for in the budget resolution.

At the end of December 2005, Secretary of the Treasury Snow wrote Congress that the debt limit would probably be reached in mid-February 2006, although the Treasury could take actions that maintain the debt below its limit until mid-March. He therefore requested an increase in the debt limit.[57] In two more letters, sent on February 19 and March 6, Secretary Snow advised Congress that the Treasury was taking measures within its legal discretion to avoid reaching the limit and that these measures would suffice only until the middle of March 2006. Secretary Snow authorized actions used previously by the Treasury, including declaring a debt issuance suspension period. As March began, the government was again close to becoming unable to meet its obligations. During the week of March 13 the Senate took up H.J.Res. 47. On March 16, the Senate passed a debt limit increase after rejecting several amendments. The President's signature on March 20, 2006, then raised the debt limit (P.L. 109-182) to $8,965 billion.

In mid-May 2007, Congress passed the conference report (H.Rept. 110-153) on the FY2008 budget resolution. The House's Gephardt rule, triggered by the adoption of the conference report on the budget resolution, resulted in the automatic engrossment of a joint resolution (in this case, H.J.Res. 43, 110th Congress) raising the debt limit by $850 billion to $9,815 billion, and sending it to the Senate. At the end of July 2007, the Treasury asked Congress to raise the debt limit, stating the limit would be reached in early October 2007. In August, the CBO Director said that projections suggested that the limit would be reached in late October or early November. Without an increase, the Treasury indicated that it would take steps within its legal authority to avoid exceeding the debt limit. The Senate Finance Committee approved the House resolution (H.J.Res. 43) without changes on September 12, 2007. The Senate then passed the measure on September 27, which the President signed on September 29, 2007 (P.L. 110-91).

The Economic Slowdown and Federal Debt

Fiscal Policy Considerations

The U.S. economy is currently recovering slowly from a severe economic recession that began in December 2007 and ended in June 2009.[58] The economic slowdown began with a rapid deceleration of housing prices and a rise in interest rate spreads between private lending rates and benchmark Federal Reserve rates, indicating an increasing reluctance of major financial institutions to lend to each other as well as to firms and individuals. This led to sharply higher federal deficit spending in FY2008 spurred by several major actions taken by Congress to unfreeze credit markets, boost consumption, and increase spending. Deficit spending was even higher in FY2009, with higher than average deficits as a percentage of GDP persisting into the next decade, likely leading to further increases in the federal debt and debt limit. While deficits for FY2010 were slightly lower and fiscal conditions are projected to improve in FY2011, deficits remain high relative to historical experience.

Economic recession affects the federal deficit in several ways. First, falling prices of many assets and equities can sharply reduce federal revenues from capital gains taxes and from the corporate tax. Second, individual income taxes, the largest component of federal revenues, may also fall if jobs are cut and unemployment increases due to economic conditions. Third, "automatic stabilizers" such as unemployment insurance and income support programs pay out more money as unemployment rises and the number of households eligible for means-tested benefits rises, thus increasing federal spending.

Boosting the economy through deficit spending provides a fiscal stimulus if the output levels of goods and services produced in the nation are below their potential levels. Deficit spending, however, can help accelerate inflation if output levels are near or at potential levels, and in addition, exacerbates long-term fiscal challenges. Several economists have expressed concerns that inflation, which had been relatively low since the early 1980s, could accelerate due to rising prices of food, energy, and primary commodities. While inflation would reduce the market value of the federal deficit, it would require Treasury to pay higher nominal interest rates on federal debt. The U.S. economy, however, is currently operating well below its potential, which has kept inflation at lower levels.

Raising the Debt Ceiling in 2008, 2009, and 2010

In a March 2008 report, CBO estimated the President's budget would lead to a $396 billion deficit in FY2008 and a $342 billion deficit in FY2009.[59] The actual deficit for FY2008 reached $455 billion. In August 2009, CBO estimated the deficit would total $1,587 billion in FY2009 and $1,381 billion in FY2010.[60] As a result of the current economic conditions and the actions of the federal government to bring the economy out of recession, the federal debt limit was raised twice in the second half of 2008 and twice in 2009.

The House Concurrent Resolution on the Budget (H.Con.Res. 312) recommended policies that would result in a $10,200 billion debt in FY2009. The Senate Concurrent Resolution on the Budget S.Con.Res. 70) recommended policies that would result in a total debt of $10,278 billion in FY2009.[61] Implementing either set of policies would require an increase in the federal debt limit. The conference agreement (H.Rept. 110-659) also recommended spending levels that would lead to a debt subject to limit of $10,207 billion in FY2009, a level that would require an increase in the statutory debt limit. The budget conference report passed the Senate on a 48-45 vote on June 4, 2008. The House passed the measure on the next day by a 214-210 vote. Agreement on the FY2009 budget resolution automatically created and deemed passed in the House legislation (H.J.Res. 92) that would increase the debt limit from its current level of $9,815 billion to $10,615 billion. Because the Senate did not take up H.J.Res. 92, the debt limit remained at $9,815 billion.

Subsequently, the House passed an amended version of the Housing and Economic Recovery Act of 2008 (H.R. 3221) by a vote of 272-152 that included a debt limit increase to $10,615 billion on July 23, 2008. The Senate then passed the measure on July 26 on a 72-13 vote. The President signed the bill on July 30 (P.L. 110-289), increasing the debt limit. In addition to increasing the debt limit, the act also contained provisions that would temporarily authorize the Secretary of Treasury to extend a line of credit to mortgage guarantee agencies Freddie Mac and Fannie Mae. The act also created the a new independent agency called the Federal Housing Finance Agency (FHFA), which replaced the Department of Housing and Urban Development Office of Federal Housing Enterprise Oversight (OFHEO) and the Federal Housing Finance Board (FHFB).

While CBO indicated that it was more likely than not that such intervention would not be needed, it also estimated a 5% chance of a cost to taxpayers of more than $100 billion.[62] Because debt subject to limit was just $339 billion less than the debt ceiling of $9,815 billion when the Senate passed H.R. 3221, some financial market participants may have worried that the debt limit, without an increase, might have hindered the Treasury Secretary's ability to intervene to support Freddie Mac and Fannie Mae. On September 7, 2008, the FHFA placed Fannie Mae and Freddie Mac in conservatorship, providing FHFA with the full powers to control the assets and operations of the firms.

Since the deprivatization of Fannie Mae and Freddie Mac, the federal government has acted to provide stability to financial markets.[63] On September 20, 2008, the U.S. Treasury submitted a proposal to Congress to authorize the Treasury Secretary to buy mortgage-related assets in order to stabilize financial markets. The Treasury proposal would allow Treasury holdings of mortgage-related securities up to $700 billion and would raise the debt limit to $11,315 billion.[64]

Representative Barney Frank proposed an amendment (Emergency Economic Stabilization Act of 2008) to a vehicle measure (H.R. 3997) that incorporated the main tenets of the Treasury proposal including raising the debt limit to $11,315 billion.[65] On September 29, 2008, however, the House rejected that amendment.

On October 1, 2008, the Senate voted on, and passed, a different version of the Emergency Economic Stabilization Act of 2008 (H.R. 1424) that included the same debt limit increase.[66] The House passed H.R. 1424 on October 3, 2008, and it was signed into law by the President (P.L. 110-343) on the same day, raising the debt limit to $11,315 billion.

Current economic conditions led Congress to consider another economic stimulus measure. This measure contains both tax cuts and spending increases, which will increase the deficit by reducing revenues and increasing outlays. The American Recovery and Reinvestment Act of 2009 (ARRA) as passed by the Senate on February 10, 2009 (Division B of the Senate Substitute amendment to H.R. 1 and S. 350), contained a provision which would raise the debt limit to $12,140 billion. The version of this legislation originally passed by the House omitted this provision. The final conference agreement on ARRA was passed by the House and Senate on February 13, 2009, and signed by the President on February 17, 2009 (P.L. 111-5). This measure contained a provision increasing the debt limit to $12,104 billion.

The conference report on the Concurrent Resolution on the Budget for FY2010 (S.Con.Res. 13) recommended policies that would lead to a debt subject to limit of $13,233 billion in FY2010, a level that would require an increase in the statutory debt limit. The budget resolution also contained a revised estimate of debt subject to limit of $12,016 billion for FY2009. The adoption of this conference report on April 29, 2009, triggered the Gephardt rule (House Rule XXVII), producing a House Joint Resolution (H.J.Res. 45) that would raise the debt limit by $925 billion to $13,029 billion. Under the rule, the resolution was automatically deemed passed by the House and sent to the Senate.

In August 2009, according to media reports, Secretary of Treasury Timothy Geithner notified Congress that the debt limit would be reached in mid-October.[67] On November 4, the U.S. Treasury announced that it could postpone the time when federal debt would reach its statutory limit until the middle or the end of December.[68] Treasury dropped nearly $185 billion from its balance sheet by reducing the amount of loans available through the Supplemental Financing Program, an emergency loan program created in the days following Lehman Brothers' bankruptcy, from $200 billion to $15 billion, which extended the time until the debt limit would be reached.[69] According to media reports, the Obama Administration also contemplated scaling back the Troubled Asset Relief Program (TARP), which could also lower federal debt subject to statutory limit. Repayments of TARP funds by major financial institutions could also lower the amount of debt subject to limit.[70] Other measures, such as those taken in 2003 during a "debt issuance suspension period" (described above), could also have extended the U.S. Treasury's ability to operate within the debt limit. On the other hand, the U.S. Treasury was scheduled to issue $48 billion of nonmarketable securities to the FDIC on December 30 and to make interest payments to various federal trust funds on December 31 totaling about $100 billion, according to Wall Street analysts, which in the absence of a debt limit increase, could have challenged

Treasury's debt management activities in the absence of special accounting measures.[71]

In mid-December, according to media reports, senior Members of the House chose to forgo a larger increase in the debt limit in favor of a smaller increase in the debt limit that would allow the U.S. Treasury Department to continue normal debt management operations for two months or so.[72] H.R. 4314, a measure to raise the debt limit to $12,394 billion, was introduced on December 15, 2009, and passed by the House the next day on a 218-214 vote. The Senate passed it on December 24 by a 60-39 vote, and the President signed the measure on December 28. On January 28, the Senate passed an amended version of H.J.Res. 45 on a 60-39 vote. The measure would raise the debt ceiling by $1,900 billion, to $14,294 billion.[73] In addition, one amendment to impose certain pay-as-you-go (PAYGO) restrictions was approved on a 60-40 vote.[74]

Some Members of Congress have called for the creation of a national commission to address federal debt and the government's fiscal situation, which could be enabled through a measure linked to an increase in the debt limit.[75] An amendment (S.Amdt. 3302 to S.Amdt. 3299) to H.J.Res. 45 that would have established a "Bipartisan Task Force for Responsible Fiscal Action" was not approved on a 53-46 vote, having failed to reach 60 votes, on January 26, 2010. President Obama then charged a National Commission on Fiscal Responsibility and Reform (Fiscal Commission) with identifying "policies to improve the fiscal situation in the medium term and to achieve fiscal sustainability over the long run."[76] The Fiscal Commission issued a report on December 1, 2010, and several commissioners issued their own fiscal proposals as well.[77]

The House approved H.J.Res. 45 on a 233-187 vote on February 4, forwarding the measure to the President. The Obama Administration had previously voiced its strong support for a debt limit increase.[78] The President signed the measure (P.L. 111-139) on February 12, 2010.

Raising the Debt Ceiling in 2011

On May 16, 2011, U.S. Treasury Secretary Timothy Geithner announced that the federal debt had reached its statutory limit and declared a debt issuance suspension period, which would allow certain extraordinary measures to extend Treasury's borrowing capacity until about August 2, 2011.[79] On July 1, 2011, the U.S. Treasury confirmed its view that its borrowing authority would be exhausted on that day.[80]

While many of the extraordinary measures have been used by previous Treasury Secretaries, the funding provided by those measures may buy much less time than in previous debt limit episodes. Given the size of the FY2011 federal deficit, projected to reach $1,399 billion according to the latest Congressional Budget Office (CBO) baseline estimates, those extraordinary measures may provide limited additional time before the federal government becomes unable to meet its financial obligations.[81]

On July 15, the U.S. Treasury announced that it had suspended reinvestment in the Exchange Stabilization Fund, one of the last available extraordinary measures before its borrowing authority (according to Treasury projections) would be exhausted on August 2.[82] One analyst, who had not expected this step to be taken until August 1, stated that the U.S. Treasury may have less headroom for cash management than previously anticipated.[83] Thus, funding federal operations could soon become increasingly complicated without a debt limit increase.[84] An independent analysis of Treasury cash flows, based on imputations from past Treasury reports, projects that from August 3 through the end of the month, cash inflows would total $174.4 billion, about $134.3 billion less than projected outflows of $306.7 billion.[85] Cash flow projections are subject to significant uncertainties.

Treasury estimates of when the debt limit would begin to bind and how long extraordinary measures would suffice to meet federal obligations have shifted since the Treasury Secretary's January 6, 2011, letter to Congress requesting a debt limit increase. Higher individual income tax revenues helped expand the headroom between the federal debt and its limit in late April. Sales of mortgage-backed securities (MBSs) also provided a relatively small amount of additional headroom. Estimates calculated by others of when Treasury would reach the debt limit and how long extraordinary measures would extend federal borrowing capacity have typically been close to Treasury's estimates.[86] Such estimates require analysis of federal spending patterns, the pace of federal debt redemptions and refinancings, and the inflow of receipts, each of which is subject to uncertainties.

The Treasury Secretary, in a letter to Congress dated May 2, 2011, had indicated that he would declare a debt issuance suspension period on May 16, unless Congress acted beforehand, which would allow certain extraordinary measures to extend Treasury's borrowing capacity until early August 2011.[87] Certain measures that rely on the Treasury Secretary's existing authority, such as the draw-down of the Supplementary Financing Program (SFP), have already taken place. The SFP, an initiative intended to help manage monetary policy, had been drawn down from $200 billion to $5 billion to provide additional headroom under the limit.[88] New issues of State and Local Government Series (SLGS) Treasury securities were suspended on May 6, 2011.

On January 6, 2011, Treasury Secretary Geithner sent a letter to Senate Majority Leader Harry Reid requesting an increase in the debt limit. At that time, Secretary Geithner stated that federal debt would likely reach its statutory limit between March 31 and May 16, 2011.[89] On April 4, the Treasury Secretary wrote Congress that estimates indicated that federal debt would reach its limit between April 15 and May 31, 2011.[90] The U.S. Treasury had also previously projected that its borrowing capacity, even using extraordinary measures, would be exhausted about July 8, 2011.[91]

On July 25, 2011, legislation titled the Budget Control Act of 2011 was introduced in different forms by both House Speaker Boehner (House Substitute Amendment to S. 627) and Majority Leader Reid (S.Amdt. 581 to S. 1323). Subsequently, on August 2, 2011, President Obama signed into law a compromise measure (P.L. 112-25), following House approval by a vote of 269-161 on August 1, 2011, and Senate approval by a vote of 74-26 on August 2, 2011. Included in this measure were numerous provisions aimed at deficit reduction and an increase in the debt limit of up to $2.4 trillion that would occur in several stages. These provisions would eliminate the need for further increases in the debt limit until late 2012 or early 2013.

Deficit Estimates

The size of the debt may remain a concern in the future due to the size of impending federal deficits necessitating further increases in the debt limit. CBO warns that the current trajectory of federal borrowing is unsustainable and could lead to slower economic growth in the long run as debt rises as a percentage of GDP. The total federal deficit rose from $455 billion in FY2008 to $1,413 billion in FY2009, and fell slightly to $1,294 billion in FY2010.[92] Much of the increase in deficits can be attributed to weak economic and financial market turmoil that started in late 2007, as well as to federal responses. Nonetheless, many budget experts remain concerned that a slow economic recovery or a "double-dip" recession could keep federal revenues below previous trendline projections for several years, and that the federal government would continue to run large deficits.

Table 2 summarizes the increases in the debt limit from 1993-2010.[93]

Table 2. Increases in the Debt Limit 1993-2010

Date	Public Law (P.L.) Number	New Debt Limit ($ billion)	Change From Previous Limit ($ billion)
April 6, 1993	P.L. 103-12	$4,370[a]	$225
August 10, 1993	P.L. 103-66	4,900	530
February 8, 1996	P.L. 104-103	([b])	—
March 12, 1996	P.L. 104-115	([c])	—
March 29, 1996	P.L. 104-121	5,500	600[d]
August 5, 1997	P.L. 105-33	5,950	450
June 28, 2002	P.L. 107-199	6,400	450
May 27, 2003	P.L. 108-24	7,384	984
November 19, 2004	P.L. 108-415	8,184	800
March 20, 2006	P.L. 109-182	8,965	781
September 29, 2007	P.L.110-91	9,815	850
July 30, 2008	P.L. 110-289	10,615	800
October 3, 2008	P.L. 110-343	11,315	700
February 17, 2009	P.L. 111-5	12,104	789
December 28, 2009	P.L. 111-123	12,394	290
February 12, 2010	P.L. 111-139	14,294	1,900

Sources: CRS, compiled using the Legislative Information System, available at http://www.congress; OMB.

[a] Increased the debt limit temporarily through September 30, 1993.

[b] Temporarily exempted from limit obligations in an amount equal to the monthly insurance benefits payable under Title II of the Social Security Act in March 1996, the exemption to expire on the earlier of an increase in the limit or March 15, 1996.

[c] Temporarily exempted from limit (a) obligations in an amount equal to the monthly insurance benefits payable under Title II of the Social Security Act in March 1996 and (b) certain obligations issued to trust funds and other Federal Government accounts, both exemptions to expire on the earlier of an increase in the limit or March 30, 1996.

[d] Difference from debt limit set on August 10, 1983.

CONCLUDING COMMENTS

Since the late 1950s, the federal government increased its borrowing from the public in all years, except in FY1969 following imposition of a war surcharge and in the period FY1997-FY2001. The persistence of federal budget deficits has required the government to issue more and more debt to the public.[94] The accumulation of Social Security and other trust funds, particularly after 1983 when recommendations of the Greenspan Commission were implemented, led to sustained growth in government-held debt subject to limit.[95] The growth in federal debt held by the public and in intergovernmental accounts, such as trust funds, has periodically obliged Congress to raise the debt limit.

Between August 1997, when the debt limit was raised to $5,950 billion, and the beginning of FY2002 in October 2001, federal budget surpluses reduced debt held by the public. In early 2001, the 10-year budget forecasts projected large and growing surpluses, indicating rapid reduction in debt held by the public. Some experts expressed concern about consequences of retiring all federal debt held by the public.[96] Most long-term forecasts computed at that time, however, showed large deficits emerging once the baby boomers began to retire. Short-term forecasts projected continuous growth in debt held by government accounts, largely due to the difference between Social Security tax revenues and benefit payments. The combination of falling levels of publicly held debt and rising levels of debt held by government accounts moderated the expected growth of total debt. The moderate growth in total debt those projections had forecast was expected to postpone the need to increase the debt limit until late into the decade, when accumulating debt in government accounts would overtake reductions in debt held by the public.

New budget projections released in early 2002 smashed expectations of large, persistent surpluses, and hopes for reductions in debt held by the public collapsed. The return to large federal deficits accelerated the growth of total debt, necessitating increases in the debt limit. Debate during the most recent debt limit increases has shown a growing concern with the fiscal sustainability. Over the next decade, without major changes in federal policies, persistent and possibly growing deficits, along with the ongoing growth in the debt holdings of government accounts, would increase substantially the amount of federal debt subject to limit. Unless federal policies change, Congress would repeatedly face demands to raise the debt limit to accommodate the growing federal debt in order to provide the government with the means to meet its financial obligations.

FURTHER READING

Drishnakumar, Anita S., "In Defense of the Debt Limit Statute," *Harvard Journal on Legislation*, vol. 42, 2005, pp. 135-185.

Gordon, John Steele, *Hamilton's Blessing: the Extraordinary Life and Times of Our National Debt*, New York: Penguin, 1998.

Hormats, Robert D., *The Price of Liberty: Paying for America's Wars from the Revolution to the War on Terror*, New York: Times Books, 2007.

Noll, Franklin, "The United States Public Debt, 1861 to 1975," EH.Net Encyclopedia, edited by Robert Whaples, May 26, 2004. Available at http://eh.net/encyclopedia/article/noll.publicdebt.

Wright, Robert E., *One Nation Under Debt: Hamilton, Jefferson, and the History of What We Owe*, New York: McGraw-Hill, 2008.

Appendix A. Debt Subject to Limit by Month Since September 2001

Table A-1 provides data on the dollar amount, in current dollars, of federal debt and the changes in these amounts by month between the end of September 2001 (the end of FY2001) and the end of December 2010. The table shows outstanding monthly balances, subject to the debt limit, of total federal debt, debt held by government accounts, and debt held by the public.

All three measures of debt subject to limit increased over this period. From the end of September 2001 (the end of FY2001) to the end of September 2010 (the most recently completed fiscal year), total federal debt increased by $7,778 billion, debt held in government accounts increased by $2,073 billion, and debt held by the public increased by $5,705 billion. All three measures experienced periodic reductions in some months. Because federal receipts and outlays are spread unevenly over the fiscal year, debt may rise or fall in a given month, even if debt measures follow an overall increasing trend.

Table A-1. Debt Subject to Limit by Month, September 2001-December 2010 (in millions of current dollars)

End of Month	Total	Change From Previous Period	Held by Government Accounts	Change From Previous Period	Held by the Public	Change From Previous Period
Sept. 2001	$5,732,802	—	$2,436,521	—	$3,296,281	—
Oct. 2001	5,744,523	$11,721	2,451,815	$15,294	3,292,709	$-3,572
Nov. 2001	5,816,823	72,300	2,469,647	17,832	3,347,176	54,467
Dec. 2001	5,871,413	54,590	2,516,012	46,365	3,355,401	8,225
Jan. 2002	5,865,892	-5,521	2,525,755	9,743	3,340,138	-15,263

End of Month	Total	Change From Previous Period	Held by Government Accounts	Change From Previous Period	Held by the Public	Change From Previous Period
Feb. 2002	5,933,154	67,262	2,528,494	2,739	3,404,659	64,521
Mar. 2002	5,935,108	1,954	2,528,318	-176	3,406,789	2,130
Apr. 2002	5,914,816	-20,292	2,549,438	21,120	3,365,378	-41,411
May 2002	5,949,975	35,159	2,553,350	3,912	3,396,625	31,247
June 2002	6,058,313	108,338	2,630,646	77,296	3,427,667	31,042
July 2002	6,092,050	33,737	2,627,980	-2,666	3,464,070	36,403
Aug. 2002	6,142,835	50,785	2,620,946	-7,034	3,521,890	57,820
Sept. 2002	6,161,431	18,596	2,644,244	23,298	3,517,187	-4,703
Oct. 2002	6,231,284	69,853	2,680,812	36,568	3,550,472	33,285
Nov. 2002	6,294,480	63,196	2,680,788	-24	3,613,692	63,220
Dec. 2002	6,359,412	64,932	2,745,787	64,999	3,613,625	-67
Jan. 2003	6,355,812	-3,600	2,753,301	7,514	3,602,511	-11,114
Feb. 2003	6,399,975	44,163	2,750,471	-2,830	3,649,504	46,993
Mar. 2003	6,399,975	0	2,722,812	-27,659	3,677,163	27,659
Apr. 2003	6,399,975	0	2,731,042	8,230	3,668,933	-8,230
May 2003	6,498,658	98,683	2,755,895	24,853	3,742,763	73,830
June 2003	6,625,519	126,861	2,842,361	86,466	3,783,158	40,395
July 2003	6,704,814	79,295	2,835,566	-6,795	3,869,247	86,089
Aug. 2003	6,743,775	38,961	2,829,387	-6,179	3,914,388	45,141
Sept. 2003	6,737,553	-6,222	2,846,730	17,343	3,890,823	-23,565
Oct. 2003	6,826,668	89,115	2,869,493	22,763	3,957,175	66,352
Nov. 2003	6,879,626	52,958	2,879,117	9,624	4,000,509	43,334
Dec. 2003	6,952,893	73,267	2,940,736	61,619	4,012,157	11,648
Jan. 2004	6,966,851	13,958	2,951,219	10,483	4,015,633	3,476
Feb. 2004	7,049,163	82,312	2,953,123	1,904	4,096,040	80,407
Mar. 2004	7,088,648	39,485	2,941,195	-11,928	4,147,453	51,413
Apr. 2004	7,089,700	1,052	2,960,151	18,956	4,129,549	-17,904
May 2004	7,151,523	61,823	2,973,869	13,718	4,177,653	48,104
June 2004	7,229,320	77,797	3,039,987	66,118	4,189,334	11,681
July 2004	7,271,328	42,008	3,033,396	-6,591	4,237,933	48,599
Aug. 2004	7,305,531	34,203	3,037,149	3,753	4,268,382	30,449
Sept. 2004	7,333,350	27,819	3,056,590	19,441	4,276,760	8,378
Oct. 2004	7,383,975	50,625	3,096,207	39,617	4,287,768	11,008
Nov. 2004	7,464,740	80,765	3,087,834	-8,373	4,376,906	89,138
Dec. 2004	7,535,644	70,904	3,158,531	70,697	4,377,114	208
Jan. 2005	7,567,702	32,058	3,171,089	12,558	4,396,615	19,501
Feb. 2005	7,652,726	85,024	3,176,406	5,317	4,476,320	79,705
Mar. 2005	7,715,503	62,777	3,175,460	-946	4,540,042	63,722
Apr. 2005	7,704,041	-11,462	3,185,364	9,904	4,518,677	-21,365
May 2005	7,717,574	13,533	3,207,232	21,868	4,510,342	-8,335
June 2005	7,778,128	60,554	3,280,914	73,682	4,497,214	-13,128
July 2005	7,829,029	50,901	3,278,725	-2,189	4,550,304	53,090
Aug. 2005	7,868,395	39,366	3,284,696	5,971	4,583,699	33,395
Sept. 2005	7,871,040	2,645	3,300,969	16,273	4,570,071	-13,628
Oct. 2005	7,964,782	93,742	3,345,589	44,620	4,619,193	49,122

Table A-1. (Continued)

End of Month	Total	Change From Previous Period	Held by Government Accounts	Change From Previous Period	Held by the Public	Change From Previous Period
Nov. 2005	8,028,918	64,136	3,351,093	5,504	4,677,826	58,633
Dec. 2005	8,107,019	78,101	3,424,304	73,211	4,682,715	4,889
Jan. 2006	8,132,290	25,271	3,442,543	18,239	4,689,747	7,032
Feb. 2006	8,183,975	51,685	3,457,409	14,866	4,726,567	36,820
Mar. 2006	8,281,451	97,476	3,443,602	-13,807	4,837,849	111,282
Apr. 2006	8,262,718	-18,733	3,479,623	36,021	4,783,095	-54,754
May 2006	8,263,812	1,094	3,492,648	13,025	4,771,165	-11,930
June 2006	8,330,646	66,834	3,566,186	73,538	4,764,460	-6,705
July 2006	8,352,614	21,968	3,569,550	3,364	4,783,064	18,604
Aug. 2006	8,423,321	70,707	3,576,166	6,616	4,847,155	64,091
Sept. 2006	8,420,278	-3,043	3,622,378	46,212	4,828,972	-18,183
Oct. 2006	8,498,016	77,738	3,650,241	27,863	4,847,775	18,803
Nov. 2006	8,545,715	47,699	3,649,736	-505	4,895,979	48,204
Dec. 2006	8,592,513	46,798	3,724,450	74,714	4,868,063	-27,916
Jan. 2007	8,619,499	26,986	3,737,894	13,444	4,881,605	13,542
Feb. 2007	8,690,921	71,422	3,744,299	6,405	4,946,622	65,017
Mar. 2007	8,760,735	69,814	3,740,127	-4,172	5,020,608	73,986
Apr. 2007	8,753,070	-7,665	3,778,255	38,128	4,974,815	-45,793
May 2007	8,740,892	-12,178	3,792,201	13,946	4,948,691	-26,124
June 2007	8,779,168	38,276	3,867,819	75,618	4,911,348	-37,343
July 2007	8,845,417	66,249	3,873,239	5,420	4,972,178	60,830
Aug. 2007	8,918,493	73,076	3,854,115	-19,124	5,064,377	92,199
Sept. 2007	8,921,343	2,850	3,903,710	49,595	5,017,633	-46,744
Oct. 2007	8,994,639	73,296	3,958,357	54,647	5,036,281	18,648
Nov. 2007	9,065,827	71,188	3,950,468	-7,889	5,115,358	79,077
Dec. 2007	9,144,715	78,888	4,038,566	88,098	5,106,149	-9,209
Jan. 2008	9,155,842	11,127	4,053,199	14,633	5,102,644	-3,505
Feb. 2008	9,275,683	119,841	4,045,007	-8,192	5,230,676	128,032
Mar. 2008	9,358;135	82,452	4,051,685	6,678	5,306,450	75,774
Apr. 2008	9,298,567	-59,568	4,080,887	29,202	5,217,680	-88,770
May 2008	9,324,137	25,570	4,071,992	-8,895	5,252,144	34,464
June 2008	9,427,901	167,869	4,169,509	134,950	5,258,392	32,920
July 2008	9,520,220	92,319	4,144,377	-25,132	5,375,843	117,451
Aug. 2008	9,580,508	60,288	4,129,413	-14,964	5,451,095	75,252
Sept. 2008	9,959,850	379,342	4,179,574	50,161	5,780,276	329,181
Oct. 2008	10,504,702	544,852	4,231,878	52,304	6,272,824	492,548
Nov. 2008	10,595,725	91,023	4,228,270	-3,608	6,367,454	94,630
Dec. 2008	10,640,274	44,549	4,298,482	70,212	6,341,792	-25,662
Jan. 2009	10,569,310	-70,964	4,278,424	-20,058	6,290,886	-50,906
Feb. 2009	10,814,630	245,320	4,261,734	-16,690	6,552,896	262,010
Mar. 2009	11,066,217	251,587	4,258,272	-3,462	6,807,946	255,050
Apr. 2009	11,178,827	112,610	4,273,005	14,733	6,905,822	97,876

End of Month	Total	Change From Previous Period	Held by Government Accounts	Change From Previous Period	Held by the Public	Change From Previous Period
May 2009	11,260,445	81,618	4,265,719	-7,286	6,994,725	88,903
June 2009	11,487,470	227,025	4,336,673	70,954	7,150,797	156,072
July 2009	11,611,178	123,708	4,299,673	-37,000	7,311,505	160,708
Aug. 2009	11,755,205	144,027	4,294,923	-4,750	7,460,282	148,777
Sept. 2009	11,853,434	98,229	4,325,124	30,201	7,528,311	68,029
Oct. 2009	11,836,629	-16,805	4,372,308	47,184	7,464,321	-63,990
Nov. 2009	12,057,363	220,734	4,367,935	-4,373	7,689,428	225,107
Dec. 2009	12,254,506	197,143	4,466,279	98,344	7,788,227	98,799
Jan. 2010	12,222,507	-31,999	4,485,502	19,223	7,737,005	-51,222
Feb. 2010	12,383,717	161,210	4,469,373	-16,129	7,914,344	177,339
Mar. 2010	12,716,511	332,794	4,448,645	-20,728	8,267,866	353,522
Apr. 2010	12,892,729	176,218	4,480,458	31,813	8,412,271	144,405
May 2010	12,992,539	99,810	4,498,120	17,662	8,494,419	82,148
June 2010	13,149,560	157,021	4,537,716	39,596	8,611,844	117,425
July 2010	13,185,208	35,648	4,504,601	-33,115	8,680,607	68,763
Aug. 2010	13,398,794	213,586	4,493,418	-11,183	8,905,376	224,769
Sept. 2010	13,510,840	112,046	4,509,632	16,214	9,001,208	95,832
Oct. 2010	13,617,337	106,497	4,568,895	59,263	9,048,442	47,234
Nov. 2010	13,809,121	191,784	4,555,396	-13,499	9,253,725	205,283
Dec. 2010	13,972,513	163,392	4,603,888	48,492	9,368,625	114,900

Sources: U.S. Treasury, Bureau of the Public Debt, Monthly Statement of the Public Debt, Sept. 2001-Nov. 2010, available at http://www.treasurydirect.gov /govt/reports/pd/mspd/mspd.htm; CRS calculations. Dec. 2010 data computed from Daily Treasury Statement.

APPENDIX B. MAJOR DEBT MEASURES BEFORE THE ENTRY OF UNITED STATES INTO WORLD WAR II

Table B-1. Major Federal Debt Measures, 1898-1941

Statutes at Large	Title	Bill	Public Law
30 Stat. 448	War Revenue Act of June 13, 1898	H.R. 10100	n.a.
32 Stat. 481	Spooner Act of June 28, 1902	—	n.a.
36 Stat. 11	Payne-Aldrich Tariff Act of August 5, 1909	H.R. 1438	P.L. 61-5
40 Stat. 35	First Liberty Bond Act of April 24, 1917	H.R. 2762	P.L. 65-3
40 Stat. 288	Second Liberty Bond Act of September 24, 1917	H.R. 5901	P.L. 65-43
40 Stat. 502	Third Liberty Bond Act of April 4, 1918	H.R. 1123	P.L. 65-120
40 Stat. 844	Fourth Liberty Bond Act of July 9, 1918	H.R. 12580	P.L. 65-192
40 Stat. 1309	Victory Liberty Loan Act of March 3, 1919	H.R. 16136	P.L. 65-328
42 Stat. 227	Revenue Act of November 23, 1921	H.R. 8245	P.L. 67-98
46 Stat. 19	Act of June 17, 1929	H.R. 1648	P.L. 71-11

Table B-1. (Continued)

Statutes at Large	Title	Bill	Public Law
46 Stat. 775	Act of June 17, 1930	H.R. 1244	P.L. 71-376
46 Stat. 1506	Act of March 3, 1931	H.R. 16111	P.L. 71-820
48 Stat. 337	Gold Reserve Act of January 30, 1934	H.R. 6976	P.L. 73-87
49 Stat. 20	Act of February 4, 1935	H.R. 4304	P.L. 74-3
52 Stat. 447	Act of May 26, 1938	H.R. 10535	P.L. 75-552
53 Stat. 1071	Act of July 20, 1939	H.R. 5748	P.L. 76-201
54 Stat. 516	Revenue Act of June 25, 1940	H.R. 10039	P.L. 76-656
55 Stat. 7	Revenue Act of February 19, 1941	H.R. 2959	P.L. 77-7

Source: Statutes at Large, various volumes, Kenneth D. Garbade, Birth of a Market: The U.S. Treasury Securities Market from the Great War to the Great Depression (Cambridge: MIT Press), forthcoming 2012.

Notes: Public law (P.L.) enumeration before the 1930s was not as consistently or commonly used as at present. Table 7.3 of the FY2012 Budget Historical Tables volume lists measures since 1940 (available at http://www.whitehouse.gov/sites/default/files/omb/budget/fy2012/assets/hist07z3.xls).

n.a. = not available.

End Notes

[1] Approximately 0.5% of total debt is excluded from debt limit coverage. The Treasury defines "Total Public Debt Subject to Limit" as "the Total Public Debt Outstanding less Unamortized Discount on Treasury Bills and Zero-Coupon Treasury Bonds, old debt issued prior to 1917, and old currency called United States Notes, as well as Debt held by the Federal Financing Bank and Guaranteed Debt." For details, see http://www.treasurydirect.gov. The debt limit is codified as 31 U.S.C. §3101.

[2] Although there are hundreds of trust funds, the overwhelming majority are very small. The 12 largest trust funds hold 98.8% of the federal debt held in government accounts.

[3] Other means of financing—including cash balance changes, seigniorage, and capitalization of financing accounts used to fund federal credit programs—have relatively little effect on the changes in debt held by the public.

[4] In future years, when some trust funds are projected to pay out more than they take in, funds that the Treasury would use to redeem those intergovernmental debts must be obtained via higher taxes or lower government spending.

[5] Trust fund surpluses by law must be invested in special federal government securities.

[6] For details, see CRS Report R41633, Reaching the Debt Limit: Background and Potential Effects on Government Operations, coordinated by Mindy R. Levit.

[7] Consideration of this measure began on July 25, 2011 following legislation introduced by House Speaker Boehner (House Substitute Amendment to S. 627) and Majority Leader Reid (S.Amdt. 581 to S. 1323). Speaker Boehner's proposal passed the House on July 29, 2011 by a vote of 218-210. Neither proposal passed in the Senate.

[8] Sequestration is a mechanism that directs the President to cancel budget authority or other forms of budgetary resources in order to reach specified budget reduction targets. Balanced

Budget and Emergency Deficit Control Act of 1985 (P.L. 99-177), often known as Gramm-Rudman-Hollings (GRH), introduced sequestration procedures into the federal budget process. Those sequestration procedures were modified in subsequent years to address separation of powers issues and other concerns. For details, see CRS Report R41901, Statutory Budget Controls in Effect Between 1985 and 2002, by Megan Suzanne Lynch.

[9] See CRS Report R41907, A Balanced Budget Constitutional Amendment: Background and Congressional Options , by James V. Saturno and Megan Suzanne Lynch.

[10] White House, Message from the President to the U.S. Congress, August 2, 2011, available at http://m.whitehouse.gov/the-press-office/2011/08/02/message-president-us-congress.

[11] Congress may also consider a joint resolution of disapproval for this increase.

[12] See CRS Report R41633, Reaching the Debt Limit: Background and Potential Effects on Government Operations, coordinated by Mindy R. Levit.

[13] Government Accountability Office, Debt Limit: Delays Create Debt Management Challenges and Increase Uncertainty in the Treasury Market, GAO-11-203, February 22, 2011.

[14] 31 U.S.C. §3902.

[15] 26 U.S.C. §6611.

[16] Reuters, "S&P To Deeply Cut U.S. Ratings If Debt Payment Missed," June 29, 2011. For a summary of statements by the three major ratings agencies, see CRS Report R41932, Treasury Securities and the U.S. Sovereign Credit Default Swap Market, by D. Andrew Austin and Rena S. Miller.

[17] JP Morgan Chase, "The Domino Effect of a US Treasury Technical Default," U.S. Fixed Income Strategy Group Brief, April 19, 2011; Fitch Ratings, "Thinking the Unthinkable—What if the Debt Ceiling Was Not Increased and the US Defaulted?" June 8, 2011.

[18] For details, see out-of-print CRS Report 95-1109, Authority to Tap Trust Funds and Establish Payment Priorities if the Debt Limit is not Increased, by Thomas J. Nicola and Morton Rosenberg. Available upon request from the authors. 5 U.S.C. Sec. 8348(b) defines a debt issuance suspension period as "any period for which the Secretary of the Treasury determines for purposes of this subsection that the issuance of obligations of the United States may not be made without exceeding the public debt limit." After a debt issuance suspension period ends, the Treasury Secretary must report to Congress as soon as possible regarding fund balances and any extraordinary actions taken. For details, see 5 U.S.C. Sec. 8348(j,k).

[19] U.S. Treasury, "Treasury to Begin Orderly Wind Down of Its $142 Billion Mortgage-Backed Securities Portfolio," press release, March 21, 2011, available at http://www.treasury.gov/press-center/press-releases/Pages/tg1111.aspx.

[20] Mary J. Miller, "MBS Wind Down Update—Taxpayers Have Now Recovered More than Half of Treasury's Original Investment," U.S. Treasury, Treasury Notes, May 2, 2011, available at http://www.treasury.gov/connect/blog/Pages/MBS-Wind-Down-Update-Taxpayers-Have-Now-Recovered-More-than-Half-of-Treasurys-Original-Investment.aspx.

[21] Mary Miller, Assistant Secretary of the Treasury for Financial Markets, "Federal Asset Sales Cannot Avoid Need for Increase in Debt Limit," Treasury Notes blog, May 6, 2011, available at http://www.treasury.gov/connect/blog/Pages/Federal-Asset-Sales-Cannot-Avoid-Need-for-Increase-in-Debt-Limit.aspx.

[22] U.S. General Accounting Office (GAO), Analysis of Actions Taken during the 2003 Debt Issuance Suspension Period, GAO-04-526, May 2004, available at http://www.gao.gov/new.items/d04526.pdf.

[23] For a vigorous assertion of the utility of the debt ceiling, see Anita S. Drishnakumar, "In Defense of the Debt Limit Statute," Harvard Journal on Legislation, vol. 42, 2005, pp. 135-185.

[24] Marshall A. Robinson, The National Debt Ceiling: An Experiment in Fiscal Policy, Washington, DC: The Brookings Institution, 1959, p. 5.

[25] Bruce Bartlett, "Why Congress Must Now Abolish its Debt Limit," Financial Times, October 22, 2009, p. 11; Brian C. Roseboro, Assistant Secretary for Financial Markets, U.S. Treasury, "Remarks to the Bond Market Association's Inflation-Linked Securities Conference", New York, NY, available at http://web.archive.org/web/20080709100455 /http://www.treas.gov/press/releases/js506.htm

[26] Spooner Act of June 28, 1902 (32 Stat 481; P.L. 57-183).

[27] Marshall A. Robinson, The National Debt Ceiling: An Experiment in Fiscal Policy, (Washington, DC: Brookings Institution, 1959), pp.1-6.

[28] The War Revenue Act was enacted June 13, 1898. Much of the legislative text of the act's public borrowing sections (§32, 33) were drawn from the acts of June 30, 1864, ch. 172, §1 (13 Stats. 218) and of March 3, 1865, ch. 77 (13 Stats. 469).

[29] See House debate, Congressional Record, vol. 31, part 6 (June 9, 1898), pp. 5713-5728; and Senate debate on June 10, 1898, pp. 5732-5749.

[30] P.L. 65-43, 40 Stat. 288, enacted September 24, 1917. See H. J. Cooke and M. Katzen, "The Public Debt Limit," Journal of Finance, vol. 9, no. 3 (September 1954), pp. 298-303. The Second Liberty Bond Act allowed purchases of government debt of allied (i.e., Entente) countries, which would have complicated limits on the final redemption of federal bonds issued to fund their purchase. Some federal bonds issued in the wake of the Panic of 1893 did not have maturity limits.

[31] The other acts were the Panama Canal measure (Spooner Act; P.L. 57-183), the Payne-Aldrich Tariff Act of August 5, 1909 (36 Stat 11; P.L. 61-5); and two emergency bond measures passed in March 1917 (39 Stat 1002 and 39 Stat 1021).

[32] In 1982, the debt limit was codified into 31 U.S.C. §3101 by P.L. 97-258. Subsequent changes in the debt limit have been drafted as amendments to 31 U.S.C. §3101.

[33] Middleton Beaman, a former Law Librarian of the Library of Congress, Columbia Law School professor, and advocate for the professionalization of drafting legislation, returned to Washington in 1916 to assist the House Ways and Means Committee, which originated the Liberty Bond acts and other borrowing and revenue measures. This arrangement was formalized in 1918, when the Legislative Drafting Service, the predecessor office of the modern Office of Legislative Counsel, was established. Donald R. Kennon and Rebecca M. Rodgers, The Committee on Ways and Means a Bicentennial History 1789-1989, H. Doc. 100-244, p. 258. See also, Middleton Beaman, "Bill Drafting," Law Library Journal, vol. 7 (1914), pp. 64-71. For a critical view of legislative drafting in prior decades, see James Bryce, The American Commonwealth, 3rd revised ed., vol. 1 (New York: Macmillan, 1920), chapter XV on "Congressional Legislation."

[34] Revenue Act of November 23, 1921 (42 Stat 227; P.L.67-98). See also Paul Studenski and Herman E. Kroos, Financial History of the United States, 2nd ed. (New York: McGraw-Hill, 1963), p. 316.

[35] New York Times, "President Urges Ending of Limit on Bonded Debt; Asks Congress to Facilitate Borrowing by Eliminating $30,000,000,000, 'Ceiling' Stands By Total Debt Top $45 Billion All Right for Now, Message Says—Yielding to Economizers is Seen," March 21, 1939.

[36] P.L. 76-201. See also Senate debate, Congressional Record, vol. 84, part 6 (June 1, 1939), pp. 6480, 6497-6501.

[37] This limit did not apply to certain previous public debt issues that comprised a very minor portion of the federal debt.

[38] Revenue Act of June 25, 1940 (54 Stat 516; P.L. 76-656) and Revenue Act of February 19, 1941 (55 Stat 7).

[39] U.S. Bureau of the Census, Historical Statistics of the United States: Colonial Times to 1970, H. Doc. 93-78 (Washington: GPO, 1975), Series Y 493-504.

[40] For a list of changes in the debt limit between September 1917 and 1941, see U.S. Treasury, Statistical Appendix 1980, Table 32 entitled "Debt limitation under the Second Liberty Bond Act, as amended, beginning 1917."

[41] Public Debt Acts of 1941 (P.L. 77-7), 1942 (P.L. 77-510), 1943 (78-34), 1944 (P.L. 78-333), and 1945 (P.L. 79-48).

[42] U.S. Office of Management and Budget, FY2010 Budget of the U.S. Government: Historical Tables, Table 7-3.

[43] Until 2001, Treasury publications did not divide debt subject to limit by that held by the public and that held by government accounts Table 1 uses CRS calculations that approximate levels of debt subject to limit held in these two categories for fiscal years prior to 2001.

[44] The data show components of debt compared to the size of the economy. This avoids possible distortions resulting from changing price levels over time and includes changes in per capita incomes. This percentage increases when debt grows faster than GDP and falls when it grows more slowly than GDP.

[45] Federal on-budget receipts and outlays nearly matched in FY1999, and the on-budget surplus in FY2000 was 0.9% of GDP. Prior to FY1999, the federal government last had an on-budget surplus in FY1960. Social Security receipts in excess of benefits make up most of the off-budget surplus, which has been positive since FY1985.

[46] U.S. Congress, Congressional Budget Office, An Analysis of the President's Budgetary Proposals for Fiscal Year 2009, March 2008, available at http://www.cbo.gov/ftpdocs/89xx/doc8990/03-19-AnalPresBudget.pdf.

[47] The debt limit was raised from $5,500 billion to $5,950 billion on August 5, 1997, as part of the Balanced Budget Act of 1997 (P.L. 105-33, 111 Stat. 251).

[48] For a comprehensive discussion of the Treasury's previous uses of its short-term ability to avoid breaching the debt limit, see U.S. General Accounting Office, Debt Ceiling: Analysis of Actions During the 1995-1996 Crisis, GAO/AIMD-96-130, August 1996.

[49] U.S. Department of the Treasury, Treasury News, Treasury Statement on the Debt Ceiling, May 14, 2002.

[50] For additional details, see U.S. General Accounting Office, Debt Ceiling: Analysis of Actions During the 2002 Debt Issuance Suspension Period, GAO-03-134, December 2002.

[51] Kenneth Dam, Deputy Secretary of the Treasury, letter to Speaker of the House, Dennis Hastert, December 24, 2002, available at http://www.treas.gov/press/releases/po3718.htm.

[52] The Treasury reduced the amount of debt held by selected federal accounts while it sold an equal (or smaller) amount of debt to the public. This raised cash needed to pay for ongoing obligations and kept the debt below the limit.

[53] The House Budget Committee has some discretion in setting the debt limit level in the House Joint resolution generated by the Gephardt rule. See CRS Report 98-453, Debt-Limit Legislation in the Congressional Budget Process, by Bill Heniff Jr. and CRS Report RL31913, Developing Debt-Limit Legislation: The House's "Gephardt Rule", by Bill Heniff Jr.

[54] U.S. Congress, Congressional Budget Office, The Budget and Economic Outlook: Fiscal Years 2005 to 2014, January 2004.

[55] Alan Fram, "Congress May Duck Debt Limit Raise," Oakland Tribune, June 5, 2004.

[56] John W. Snow, Secretary of the U.S. Treasury, letter to Senate Majority Leader Bill Frist, October 14, 2004, available at http://www.treas.gov/press/releases/reports/frist.pdf.

[57] John W. Snow, Secretary of the Treasury, letter to Senator Max Baucus, December 29, 2005, available at http://www.ombwatch.org/files/budget/pdf/snow_debtlimit_2006.pdf.

[58] The end of a recession is said to occur when an economy has stopped shrinking, not when it has recovered. See National Bureau of Economic Research Business Cycle Dating Committee, press release, September 20, 2010, available at http://www. nber.org/cycles/sept2010.html.

[59] U.S. Congress, Congressional Budget Office, An Analysis of the President's Budgetary Proposals for Fiscal Year 2009, Table 1.1, March 2008, available at http://www.cbo.gov/ftpdocs/89xx/doc8990/03-19-AnalPresBudget.pdf.

[59] U.S. Congress, Congressional Budget Office, The Budget and Economic Outlook: An Update, Table 1-1, August 2009, available at http://www.cbo.gov/doc.cfm?index=10521.

[60] Goldman Sachs U.S. Research, "US Daily: The Fiscal 2008 Deficit—Likely to Top $500 Billion," March 25, 2008.

[61] U.S. Congress, House Committee on the Budget, Report to Accompany H. Con. Res. 312, 110th Cong., 2nd sess., H.Rept. 110-543, March 2008, p. 99; U.S. Congress, Senate Committee on the Budget, Report to Accompany S. Res. 70, S.Prt. 110-039, March 2008.

[62] U.S. Congress, Congressional Budget Office, Cost Estimate for H.R. 3221 "Housing and Economic Recovery Act of 2008" As passed by the Senate on July 11, 2008, with an amendment transmitted to CBO on July 22, 2008, July 24, 2008, available at http://www.cbo.gov/ftpdocs/95xx/doc9597/hr3221.pdf.

[63] For additional information see CRS Report RS22956, The Cost of Government Financial Interventions, Past and Present, by Baird Webel, Marc Labonte, and N. Eric Weiss.

[64] U.S. Department of Treasury, "Fact Sheet: Proposed Treasury Authority to Purchase Troubled Assets," Press release hp-1150, September 20, 2008, available at http://www.treas.gov/press/releases/hp1150.htm.

[65] U.S. Congress, House Financial Services Committee, Emergency Economic Stabilization Act of 2008 (Amendment to the Senate Amendment to H.R. 3997), available at http://www.house.gov/apps/list/press/financialsvcs_dem/amend_001_xml.pdf. For text of debt limit provision, see Congressional Record, (September 29, 2008), p. H10355.

[66] U.S. Congress, Senate Banking, Housing, and Urban Affairs Committee, Emergency Economic Stabilization Act of 2008 (In the Nature of a Substitute to H.R. 1424), available at http://banking.senate.gov/public/_files/latestversionAYO08C32_xml.pdf.

[67] *CQ Weekly*, "Fall 2009 Outlook: Debt Limit Increase," September 7, 2009, p. 1966.

[68] U.S. Treasury, "November 2009 Quarterly Refunding Statement," press release tg346, November 4, 2009, http://www.ustreas.gov/press/releases/tg346.htm; David Clarke and CQ Staff, "Treasury Gives Congress More Breathing Room on Debt Limit," *CQ Today Online News*, November 4, 2009.

[69] For details, see Joseph Haubrich and John Lindner, "The Supplemental Financing Program," *Economic Trends,* Federal Reserve of Chicago, September 28, 2009, available at http://www.clevelandfed.org/research/trends/2009/1009/03monpol.cfm.

[70] *The Money Market Observer: Wrightson ICAP's Weekly Newsletter*, December 7, 2009.

[71] *The Money Market Observer: Wrightson ICAP's Weekly Newsletter*, November 30, 2009.

[72] Paul Kane, "House Democrats Discard Larger Debt Limit," *Washington Post*, December 15, 2009, p. A4.

[73] *CQ Today Midday Update*, "Senate Sends Debt Ceiling Increase to House," January 28, 2010.

[74] S.Amdt. 3305. A second amendment (S.Amdt. 3300), approved on a 97-0 vote, provides certain protections to the Social Security program. Other amendments were not approved.

[75] Jonathan Weisman and John D. McKinnon, "White House Weighs New Panel to Tackle Deficit: Bipartisan Commission Considered As Administration Seeks to Show Resolve on a Problem that Dogs Its Broader Agenda," *Wall Street Journal, November 26, 2009, p. A10.*

[76] Executive Order 13531, "National Commission on Fiscal Responsibility and Reform," February 18, 2010; 75 FR 7927, February 23, 2010.

[77] National Commission on Fiscal Responsibility and Reform, The Moment of Truth, report, December 1, 2010, available at http://www.fiscalcommission.gov/sites/ fiscalcommission. gov/files/documents/TheMomentofTruth12_1_2010.pdf.

[78] U.S. Office of Management and Budget, "H.J.Res. 45—Increasing the Statutory Limit on the Public Debt," Statement Of Administration Policy, January 20, 2010, available at http://www.whitehouse.gov/omb/assets/sap_111/saphjr45s_20100120.pdf.

[79] Secretary of the U.S. Treasury Timothy Geithner, letter to Majority Leader Harry Reid, dated May 16, 2011, available at http://www.treasury.gov/connect/blog/Documents/ 20110516 Letter%20to%20Congress.pdf.

[80] U.S. Treasury, "Treasury: No Change to August 2 Estimate Regarding Exhaustion of U.S. Borrowing Authority," Press release tg-1225, July 1, 2011, available at http://www. treasury.gov/press-center/press-releases/Pages/tg1225.aspx.

[81] U.S. Congressional Budget Office, "An Analysis of the President's Budgetary Proposals for Fiscal Year 2012," April 15, 2011, available at http://www.cbo.gov/doc.cfm?index=12130.

[82] U.S. Treasury, "Update: As Previously Announced, Treasury to Employ Final Extraordinary Measure to Extend U.S. Borrowing Authority Until August 2," press release TG-1243, available at http://www.treasury.gov/press-center/pressreleases/Pages/tg1243.aspx.

[83] Wrightson ICAP, The Money Market Observer, July 18, 2011.

[84] Wrightson ICAP, The Money Market Observer, May 2, 2011.

[85] Bipartisan Policy Center, "Debt Limit Analysis," June 27, 2011, available at http://www.bipartisanpolicy.org/sites/default/files/Debt%20Ceiling%20Analysis%20FINAL_0.pdf.

[86] Wrightson ICAP, The Money Market Observer, May 2, 2011; Secretary of the U.S. Treasury Timothy Geithner, letter to Majority Leader Harry Reid, dated January 6, 2011, available at http://www.treasury.gov/connect/blog/Documents/Letter.pdf.

[87] Secretary of the U.S. Treasury Timothy Geithner, letter to Speaker John Boehner, dated May 2, 2011, available at http://www.treasury.gov/connect/blog/Documents/FINAL%20 Debt% 20Limit%20Letter%2005-02-2011%20Boehner.pdf. The same text was sent to all Members.

[88] U.S. Treasury, "Treasury Announces Marketable Borrowing Estimates," press release TG-1155, May 2, 2011, available at http://www.treasury.gov/press-center/press-releases/ Pages/tg1155.aspx.

[89] Paul M. Krawzak, "Showdown Ahead on Debt Limit as Geithner Urges Action," CQ Today Online News, January 6, 2011; Secretary of the U.S. Treasury Timothy Geithner, letter to Majority Leader Harry Reid, dated January 6, 2011.

[90] U.S. Treasury, "Treasury Issues Updated Debt Limit Projections," March 1, 2011, available at http://www.treasury.gov/press-center/press-releases/Pages/tg1084.aspx.

[91] Secretary of the U.S. Treasury Timothy Geithner, letter to Majority Leader Harry Reid, dated April 4, 2011, available at http://www.treasury.gov/connect/blog/Documents /FINAL %20Letter%2004-04-2011%20Reid%20Debt%20Limit.pdf.

[92] U.S. Congressional Budget Office, The Budget and Economic Outlook: An Update, August 19, 2010, p. 1, available at http://www.cbo.gov/doc.cfm?index=11705.

[93] For a list of debt limit votes, see CRS Report R41814, Votes on Measures to Adjust the Statutory Debt Limit, 1978 to Present, by Justin Murray. For a discussion of earlier debt limit increases, see out-of-print CRS Report 98-805 E, Public Debt Limit Legislation: A Brief History and Controversies In the 1980s and 1990s, by Philip D. Winters, which is available from the authors upon request.

[94] The ability to run fiscal deficits gives the federal government useful flexibility in managing its finances, although large deficits may harm economic performance. See CRS Report RL33657, Running Deficits: Positives and Pitfalls, by D. Andrew Austin.

[95] Report of the National Commission on Social Security Reform, January 1983, available at http://www.ssa.gov/history/reports/gspan.html.

[96] Testimony of Federal Reserve Chairman Alan Greenspan, in U.S. Congress, Senate Committee on the Budget, Outlook for the Federal Budget and Implications for Fiscal Policy, hearings, 107th Cong., 1st sess., January 25, 2001, available at http://www. federalreserve.gov /boarddocs/testimony/2001/20010125/default.htm.

In: The Budget Control Act of 2011 ISBN: 978-1-61942-035-9
Editors: C. G. Lynch and C. McHale

Chapter 4

REACHING THE DEBT LIMIT: BACKGROUND AND POTENTIAL EFFECTS ON GOVERNMENT OPERATIONS*

Mindy R. Levit, Clinton T. Brass, Thomas J. Nicola, Dawn Nuschler and Alison M. Shelton

SUMMARY

The gross federal debt, which represents the federal government's total outstanding debt, consists of two types of debt: (1) debt held by the public and (2) debt held in government accounts, also known as intragovernmental debt. Federal government borrowing increases for two primary reasons: (1) budget deficits and (2) investments of any federal government account surpluses in Treasury securities, as required by law. Nearly all of this debt is subject to the statutory limit. The federal debt limit currently stands at $14,294 billion.

Treasury has yet to face a situation in which it was unable to pay its obligations as a result of reaching the debt limit. In the past, the debt limit has always been raised before the debt reached the limit. However, on several occasions Treasury took extraordinary actions to avoid reaching the limit and, as a result, affected the operations of certain programs. If

* This is an edited, reformatted and augmented version of a Congressional Research Service publication, CRS Report for Congress R41633, from www.crs.gov, dated July 27, 2011.

the Secretary of the Treasury determines that the issuance of obligations of the United States may not be made without exceeding the public debt limit, Treasury can make use of "extraordinary measures." Some of these measures require the Treasury Secretary to authorize a debt issuance suspension period.

Treasury Secretary Geithner has issued several letters to Congress concerning the debt limit. In these letters, Treasury has stated that it has an ability to delay the date by which the current debt limit would be reached by utilizing similar methods used during past crises, including declaring a debt issuance suspension period, if necessary. According to Treasury, these actions could delay the date that the debt limit would be reached by several weeks. However, if the debt limit is not raised after that point, payment of other obligations and benefits would be "discontinued, limited, or adversely affected." On May 2, 2011, Secretary Geithner stated that the debt limit would be reached no later than May 16, 2011, and that the use of extraordinary measures would extend Treasury's ability to meet commitments through August 2, 2011. On May 16, 2011, Secretary Geithner notified Congress of the beginning of a debt issuance suspension period.

Under current estimates, the federal government will have to issue an additional $738 billion in debt above the current statutory limit to finance obligations for the second half of FY2011. If the debt limit is reached and Treasury is no longer able to issue federal debt, federal spending would have to be decreased or federal revenues would have to be increased by a corresponding amount to cover the gap in what cannot be borrowed. To put this into context, the federal government would have to eliminate all spending on discretionary programs, cut nearly 70% of outlays for mandatory programs, increase revenue collection by nearly two-thirds, or take some combination of those actions in the second half of FY2011 (April through September 30, 2011) in order to avoid increasing the debt limit. Additional spending cuts and/or revenue increases would be required, under current policy, in FY2012 and beyond to avoid increasing the debt limit.

It is extremely difficult for Congress to effectively influence short-term fiscal and budgetary policy through action on legislation adjusting the debt limit. The need to raise (or lower) the limit during a session of Congress is driven by previous decisions regarding revenues and spending stemming from legislation enacted earlier in the session or in prior years. Nevertheless, the consideration of debt-limit legislation often is viewed as an opportunity to reexamine fiscal and budgetary policy. Consequently, House and Senate action on legislation adjusting the debt limit often is complicated, hindered by policy disagreements, and subject to delay.

INTRODUCTION

The federal government's statutory debt limit is currently $14,294 billion (P.L. 111-139).[1] On January 6, 2011, Secretary of the Treasury Timothy Geithner issued a letter to Congress stating that the debt limit would be reached sometime between March 31 and May 16, 2011. Treasury has subsequently revised this estimate as a result of changes in the expected levels of tax receipts, the timing of commitments and obligations, and in determining the level of cash balances needed to operate. The most recent estimate was made available in a letter issued by Secretary Geithner to Congress on May 2, 2011, which stated that the debt limit will be reached no later than May 16, 2011.[2]

On May 6 and May 16, 2011, Secretary Geithner formally notified Congress of Treasury's intent to utilize its authority outside of its typical cash management practices to pay federal obligations to delay the date by which the current debt limit would be reached (through a debt issuance suspension period as well as other methods discussed in more detail later in the report). Similar actions have been taken previously. These actions would extend Treasury's ability to meet commitments through August 2, 2011.[3] If these financing options are exhausted and Treasury is no longer able to pay for all federal obligations, some federal payments to creditors, vendors, contractors, state and local governments, beneficiaries, and other entities would be delayed or limited. This could result in significant economic and financial consequences that may have a lasting impact on federal programs and the federal government's ability to borrow in the future.

This report examines the possibility of the federal government reaching its statutory debt limit and not raising it, with a particular focus on government operations. First, the report explains the nature of the federal government's debt, the processes associated with federal borrowing, and historical events that may influence prospective actions. It also includes an analysis of what *could* happen if the federal government may no longer issue debt, has exhausted alternative sources of cash, and, therefore, depends on incoming receipts or other sources of funds to provide any cash needed to liquidate federal obligations.[4] Finally this report lays out considerations for increasing the debt limit under current policy and what impact fiscal policy could have on the debt limit going forward.

FEDERAL GOVERNMENT DEBT AND THE DEBT LIMIT[5]

The gross federal debt, which represents the federal government's total outstanding debt, consists of two types of debt:

- the debt held by the public and
- the debt held in government accounts, also known as intragovernmental debt.

Federal government borrowing increases for two primary reasons: (1) budget deficits and (2) investments of any federal government account surpluses in Treasury securities as required by law.[6]

The debt held by the public represents the total net amount borrowed from the public to cover the federal government's accumulated budget deficits. Annual budget deficits increase the debt held by the public by requiring the federal government to borrow additional funds to fulfill its commitments.

The debt held in government accounts represents the federal debt issued to certain accounts, primarily trust funds, such as those associated with Social Security, Medicare, and Unemployment Compensation. Generally, government account surpluses, which include trust fund surpluses, by law must be invested in special non-marketable federal government securities and thus are held in the form of federal debt.[7] Treasury periodically pays interest on the special securities held in a government account. Interest payments are typically paid in the form of additional special securities issued by Treasury to the trust funds, which also increases the amount of intragovernmental debt and federal debt subject to limit.

When a trust fund invests in U.S. Treasury securities, it effectively lends money to the rest of the government. The loan either reduces what the federal government must borrow from the public, if the budget is in deficit, or reduces the amount of publicly held debt, if the budget is in surplus. At the same time, the loan increases intragovernmental debt. The revenues exchanged for these securities then go into the General Fund of the Treasury and are indistinguishable from other cash in the General Fund. This cash may be used for any government spending purpose.[8]

Congress created a statutory debt limit in the Second Liberty Bond Act of 1917.[9] This development changed Treasury's borrowing process and assisted Congress in its efforts to exercise its constitutional prerogatives to control the federal government's fiscal outcomes. The debt limit also imposes a form of fiscal accountability that compels Congress and the President to take deliberate action to allow further federal borrowing if necessary.

Almost all of the federal government's borrowing is subject to a statutory limit.[10] From time to time, Congress has considered and adopted legislation to change this limit. Because the statutory limit applies to both debt held by the public and intragovernmental debt, both budget deficits and government account surpluses may contribute to the federal government reaching the existing debt limit.

THE DEBT LIMIT AND THE TREASURY

Treasury's standard methods for financing federal activities can be disrupted when the level of federal debt nears its legal limit. If the limit prevents Treasury from issuing new debt to manage short-term cash flows or to finance an annual deficit, the government may be unable to obtain the cash needed to pay its bills. The limit may also prevent the government from issuing new debt in order to invest the surpluses of designated government accounts, such as federal trust funds. Treasury is caught between two requirements: the law that requires Treasury to pay the government's legal obligations or invest trust fund surpluses, on one hand, and the statutory debt limit which may prevent Treasury from issuing the debt to raise cash to pay obligations or make trust fund investments, on the other.[11]

The level of federal debt changes throughout the year due to fluctuations in income and outlays, whether or not the government has an annual surplus or deficit. Seasonal fluctuations could still require Treasury to sell debt even if the annual level of federal debt subject to limit does not increase (i.e., if the budget were balanced and trust funds were not in surplus). Even on a day-to-day basis, the level of federal debt can vary significantly. For example, Treasury issues large volumes of individual income tax refunds in February and March, because taxpayers expecting refunds tend to file early. On the other hand, Treasury tends to collect more revenue in April because taxpayers making payments tend to file closer to April 15.

Past Treasury Secretaries, when faced with a nearly binding debt ceiling, have used special strategies to handle cash and debt management responsibilities.[12] Since 1985, these measures have included:

- suspending sales of nonmarketable debt (savings bonds, state and local government series, and other nonmarketable debt);

- trimming or delaying auctions of marketable securities;
- under-investing or disinvesting certain government funds (Social Security, Government Securities Investment Fund of the Federal Thrift Savings Plan, the Civil Service Retirement and Disability Trust Fund, Exchange Stabilization Fund); and
- exchanging Treasury securities for non-Treasury securities held by the Federal Financing Bank (FFB).

Under current law, if the Secretary of the Treasury determines that the issuance of obligations of the United States may not be made without exceeding the debt limit, a "debt issuance suspension period" may be determined.[13] This gives Treasury the authority to suspend investments in the Civil Service Retirement and Disability Trust Fund and the Government Securities Investment Fund of the Federal Thrift Savings Plan. In addition, this gives Treasury the authority to prematurely redeem securities held by the Civil Service Retirement and Disability Trust Fund. Debt issuance suspension periods were previously in effect from November 15, 1995, through January 15, 1997; April 4 through April 16, 2002; May 16 through June 28, 2002; and February 20 through May 27, 2003. On May 16, 2011, Secretary Geithner determined that a debt issuance suspension period would be in effect.[14]

Past Treasury Actions to Postpone Reaching the Debt Limit

Treasury has yet to face a situation in which it was unable to pay its obligations as a result of reaching the debt limit. However, during debt limit impasses in 1985, 1995-1996, 2002, and 2003, Treasury took extraordinary actions to avoid reaching the debt limit and to meet the federal government's other obligations. Some of the actions Treasury took during these periods are briefly discussed below, along with additional actions taken from 2009 to present.[15]

In September 1985, the Treasury Department informed Congress that it had reached the statutory debt limit. As a result, Treasury had to take extraordinary measures to meet the government's cash requirements. Treasury used various internal transactions involving the Federal Financing Bank (FFB) and delayed public auctions of government debt. It also was unable to issue, or had to delay issuing, new short-term government securities to the Civil Service Retirement and Disability Trust Fund, the Social Security Trust Funds, and several smaller trust funds. In particular, new Treasury obligations could not be issued to the trust funds because doing so would have exceeded the debt limit. Treasury took the additional step of "disinvesting" the Civil Service Retirement and Disability Trust Fund, the Social Security Trust Funds, and several smaller trust funds by redeeming some trust fund securities earlier than usual. Premature redemption of these securities created room under the debt ceiling for Treasury to borrow sufficient cash from the public to pay other obligations, including November Social Security benefits.[16] The debt limit was subsequently temporarily increased on November 14, 1985 (P.L. 99-155) and permanently increased on December 12, 1985 (P.L. 99-177) from $1,824 billion to $2,079 billion.

As a result of the 1985 debt limit crisis, Congress subsequently authorized the Treasury to alter its normal investment and redemption procedures for certain trust funds during a debt limit crisis. Such authority was not provided with respect to the Social Security trust funds. In addition, both P.L. 99-155 and P.L. 99-177 included provisions to require the Treasury to restore any interest income lost to the trust funds as a result of delayed investments and early redemptions.

During the debt limit crisis of 1995-1996, Treasury, once again, used nontraditional methods of financing, including some of the methods used during the 1985 crisis as well as not reinvesting some of the maturing Treasury securities held by the Exchange Stabilization Fund.[17] In early 1996, Treasury announced that it had insufficient cash to pay Social Security benefits for March 1996 because it was unable to issue new public debt.[18] To allow benefits to be paid in March 1996, Congress authorized the Treasury to issue securities to the public in the amount needed to make the March 1996 benefit payments and specified that, on a temporary basis, those securities would not count against the debt limit (P.L. 104-103 and P.L. 104-115). In 1996, Congress passed P.L. 104-121 to increase the debt limit and, among other provisions, to codify Congress's understanding that the Secretary of the Treasury and other federal officials are not authorized to use Social Security and Medicare funds for debt management purposes, except when necessary to provide for the payment of benefits or administrative expenses of the programs.

In addition, during periods in 2002 and 2003 (from April 4 through April 16, 2002; from May 16 through June 28, 2002; and from February 20 through May 27, 2003), Treasury again took actions to avoid reaching the debt limit, including utilizing certain trust fund assets and suspending the sale of securities to certain trust funds. The debt limit was permanently increased on

June 28, 2002 (P.L. 107-199), from $5,950 billion to $6,400 billion and on May 27, 2003 (P.L. 108-24), from $6,400 billion to $7,384 billion.

Treasury used another tool in 2009 to cope with the debt limit without declaring a debt issuance suspension period. Specifically, Treasury used a program that was originally established as an alternative method for the Federal Reserve (Fed) to increase its assistance to the financial sector during the financial downturn, the Supplementary Financing Program (SFP), which was announced on September 17, 2008. Under the SFP, Treasury temporarily auctioned more new securities than were needed to finance government operations and deposited the proceeds at the Fed. Since January 2009, the Treasury has generally held $200 billion at the Fed under this program. When debt subject to limit approached the statutory debt limit around October 2009, however, Treasury withdrew all but $5 billion from the Fed to create room under the debt ceiling. Once the debt limit was raised on February 12, 2010, from $12,394 billion to $14,294 billion (P.L. 111-139), Treasury began increasing the balances held at the Fed back to $200 billion by issuing new debt to the public. As the debt limit was approached again, the SFP was reduced from $200 billion on February 2, 2011, to $5 billion on March 3, 2011.[19]

As discussed above, short delays in increasing the debt limit have caused the Treasury Secretary to take extraordinary actions to avoid disrupting the payments of federal obligations. Though the federal government incurred additional costs during these periods, such as disruption of government borrowing and trust fund investment programs, the payment of benefits and other outlays occurred largely on schedule and trust funds were made whole once these crises ended.[20] However, if the budget continues to be in deficit and policy makers wish to avoid a default on federal obligations, such methods cannot avoid the eventual necessity of raising the debt limit.

Current Treasury Actions in 2011 Surrounding the Debt Limit

Treasury Secretary Geithner's letter to Congress of January 6, 2011, states that Treasury has an ability to delay the date by which the current debt limit would be reached by utilizing similar methods used during past crises, including declaring a debt issuance suspension period, if necessary. According to Treasury, these actions could delay the date that the debt limit would be reached by several weeks. However, if the debt limit is not raised after that point, payment of other obligations and benefits would be "discontinued, limited, or adversely affected."[21]

On April 4, 2011, Secretary Geithner issued another letter to Congress stating that the debt limit will be reached no later than May 16, 2011, and the use of extraordinary measures would extend Treasury's ability to meet commitments through July 8, 2011. Beyond these extraordinary measures discussed in the letter and detailed above, Treasury states that it does not have other actions available this year that it can take to find additional authority to issue debt. The letter further stated that the sale of certain financial assets would not be a viable option to avoid increasing the debt limit.[22]

On May 2, 2011, Secretary Geithner issued a third letter to Congress reiterating that the debt limit would be reached no later than May 16, 2011, but that the use of extraordinary measures would extend Treasury's ability to meet commitments through August 2, 2011. The revision in the latter date was a result of stronger than expected tax receipts. Further, Secretary Geithner again stated that not raising the debt limit "would have catastrophic economic impact that would be felt by every American" and that federal payments would be affected.[23] In addition, the letter stated that on Friday, May 6, the issuance of State and Local Government Series (SLGS) Treasury securities would be suspended until further notice.[24]

On May 16, 2011, Secretary Geithner notified Congress of his determination of a debt issuance suspension period and informed them of his intent to utilize additional measures related to the Civil Service Retirement and Disability Fund and the Government Securities Investment Fund (G-Fund) of the Federal Thrift Savings Plan. These funds are required by law to be made whole once the debt limit is increased. Therefore, these specific actions will not affect federal retirees or employees if the debt limit is increased.[25]

POTENTIAL IMPLICATIONS OF REACHING AND NOT RAISING THE DEBT LIMIT

If the federal government were to reach the debt limit and Treasury were to exhaust its alternative strategies for remaining under the debt limit, then the federal government would need to rely solely on incoming revenues to finance obligations. If this occurred during a period when the federal government was running a deficit, the dollar amount of newly incurred federal obligations would continually exceed the dollar amount of newly incoming revenues.

It is not possible for CRS to specifically predict what Congress, the President, the Office of Management and Budget (OMB), Treasury, federal agencies, and financial markets would do in certain situations. Nevertheless, it is possible to scope out some aspects of what *could* happen under a specific scenario, in which the federal government no longer may issue debt, has exhausted alternative sources of cash, and therefore is dependent upon incoming receipts or other sources of funds to provide any cash that is necessary to pay federal obligations. That said, CRS cannot state the full range of events that may occur if the described scenario were to actually take place.

In this scenario, the federal government implicitly would be required to use some sort of decision-making rule about whether to pay obligations in the order they are received, or, alternatively, to prioritize which obligations to pay, while other obligations would go into an unpaid queue. In other words, the federal government's inability to borrow or use other means of financing implies that payment of some or all bills or obligations would be delayed.

Possible Options for Treasury: Could Prioritization Be Used?

Some have argued that prioritization of payments can be used by Treasury to avoid a default on federal obligations by paying interest on outstanding debt before other obligations.[26] Treasury officials have maintained that the department lacks formal legal authority to establish priorities to pay obligations, asserting, in effect, that each law obligating funds and authorizing expenditures stands on an equal footing.[27] In other words, Treasury would have to make payments on obligations as they come due. With regard to this view, Treasury recently noted that an attempt to prioritize payments was "unworkable" because adopting a policy that would require certain types of payments taking precedence over other U.S. legal obligations would merely be "a failure by the U.S. to stand behind its commitments."[28]

In contrast to this view, GAO wrote to then-Chairman Bob Packwood of the Senate Finance Committee in 1985 that it was aware of no requirement that Treasury must pay outstanding obligations in the order in which they are received.[29] GAO concluded that "Treasury is free to liquidate obligations in any order it finds will best serve the interests of the United States." In any case, if Treasury were to prioritize, it is not clear what the priorities might be among the different types of spending.[30]

While the positions of Treasury and GAO may appear at first glance to differ, closer analysis suggests that they merely offer two different interpretations of Congress's silence with respect to a prioritization system for paying obligations. On one hand, GAO's 1985 opinion posits that Congress's legislative silence simply leaves the determination of payment prioritization to the discretion of the Treasury Department. Conversely, Treasury appears to assert that the lack of specific legislative direction from Congress operates as a legal barrier, effectively preventing it from establishing a prioritization system.

Possible Options for OMB: Could Apportionment Be Used?

It also is possible that OMB may use statutory authority to apportion or reapportion budget authority (i.e., the authority to incur obligations) that Congress has granted in appropriations, contract, and borrowing authority to delay expenditures and effectively establish priorities for liquidating obligations. OMB is required by statute to "apportion" these funds (e.g., quarterly) to prevent agencies from spending at a rate that would exhaust their appropriations before the end of the fiscal year.[31] If OMB were to use statutory apportionment authority to affect the rate of federal spending, its ability to do so would be constrained by the Impoundment Control Act of 1974, title X of the Congressional Budget and Impoundment Control Act of 1974 (P.L. 93-344).[32] The Impoundment Control Act does not prohibit the President from withholding funds, but establishes procedures for the President to submit formal requests to Congress either to defer (i.e., delay) spending until later or rescind (i.e., cancel) the budget authority that Congress previously had granted.[33] Although the use of OMB's apportionment authority in the event of a debt limit crisis might delay the need to pay some obligations, use of the authority would not prevent obligations from remaining unpaid.

Potential Impacts on Government Operations

If the debt limit is reached and not increased, federal spending would be affected. Under normal circumstances, Treasury has sufficient financial resources to liquidate all obligations arising from discretionary and mandatory (direct) spending, the latter of which includes interest payments on the debt.[34] If a lapse in raising the debt limit should prevent Treasury from being able to liquidate all obligations on time, it is not clear whether the distinction between different types of spending would be significant or whether the need to establish priorities would disproportionately impact one type of spending or another. It is also not clear whether the distinctions among different types of obligations, such as contract, grant, benefit, and interest payments, would prove to be significant.

Potential Impacts on Programs Generally

A government that delays paying its obligations in effect borrows from vendors, contractors, beneficiaries, other governments,[35] or employees who are not paid on time. Moreover, a backlog of unpaid bills would continue to grow until the government collects more revenues or other sources of cash than its outlays. In some cases, delaying federal payments incurs interest penalties under some statutes such as the Prompt Payment Act, which directs the government to pay interest penalties to contractors if it does not pay them by the required payment date,[36] and the Internal Revenue Code, which requires the government to pay interest penalties if tax refunds are delayed beyond a certain date.[37] The specific impacts of delayed payment would depend upon the nature of the federal program or activity for which funds are to be paid.

Potential Impacts on Programs with Trust Funds

If Treasury delays investing a federal trust fund's revenues in government securities, or redeems prematurely a federal trust fund's holdings of government securities, the result would be a loss of interest to the affected trust fund. This could potentially worsen the financial situation of the affected trust fund(s) and accelerate insolvency dates.[38] As noted earlier, Congress passed P.L. 104-121 to prevent federal officials from using the Social Security and Medicare Trust Funds for debt management purposes, except when necessary to provide for the payment of benefits and administrative expenses of the programs. Under P.L. 99-509, Treasury is permitted to delay investment in the TSP's G-Fund and the Civil Service Retirement and Disability Trust Fund, and also to redeem prematurely assets of the Civil Service Retirement and Disability Trust Fund. However, the law also requires Treasury to make these funds whole after a debt limit impasse is resolved. The government maintains a number of other trust funds whose finances could potentially be harmed by delayed investment or early redemption in the absence of similar actions to make the trust funds whole after a debt limit impasse has ended.

Distinction between a Debt Limit Crisis and a Government Shutdown

In 1995, the Congressional Budget Office (CBO) contrasted this sort of scenario, under which the debt limit is reached and not raised, with a substantially different situation, in which the government must shut down due to lack of appropriations.

> Failing to raise the debt ceiling would not bring the government to a screeching halt the way that not passing appropriations bills would. Employees would not be sent home, and checks would continue to be issued. If the Treasury was low on cash, however, there could be delays in honoring checks and disruptions in the normal flow of government services.[39]

Alternatively stated, in a situation when the debt limit is reached and Treasury exhausts its financing alternatives, aside from ongoing cash flow, an agency may continue to obligate funds. However, Treasury may not be able to liquidate all obligations that result in federal outlays due to a shortage of cash. In contrast to this, if Congress and the President do not enact interim or full-year appropriations for an agency, the agency does not have budget authority available for obligation. If this occurs, the agency must shut down non-excepted activities, with immediate effects on government services.[40]

Potential Economic and Financial Effects

In addition to the potential impact on federal programs and activities if the debt limit is not increased, there may also be economic and financial consequences. A 1979 GAO report described the consequences of failing to increase the debt ceiling. GAO said the government had never defaulted on any of its securities, because cash has been available to pay interest and redeem them upon maturity or demand.[41] Further, GAO said a default on the securities could have adverse effects on the economy, the public welfare, and the government's ability to market future securities.

> It is difficult to perceive all the adverse effects that a government default for even a short time would have on the economy and the public welfare. It is generally recognized that a default would preclude the government from honoring all of its obligations to pay for such things as employees' salaries and wages; social security benefits, civil service retirement, and other benefits from trust funds; contractual services and supplies, and maturing securities.... At a minimum, however, the government could be subject to additional claims for interest on unredeemed matured debt and to claims for damages resulting from failure to make payments. But even beyond that, the full faith and credit of the U.S. government would be threatened. Domestic

money markets, in which government securities play a major role, could be affected substantially.[42]

If the debt limit were reached and interest payments on debt were paid, it is not clear what the repercussions would be on the financial markets or the economy. If Treasury had to rely on incoming cash to pay its obligations, a significant portion of government spending would go unpaid. Removing a portion of government spending from the economy would leave behind significant economic effects and would have an effect on GDP by definition, all other things being equal.[43] Further, if the government fails to make timely payments to individuals, service providers, and other organizations, these persons and entities would also be affected. Even if the government continued paying interest, it is not clear whether creditors would retain or lose faith in the government's willingness to pay its obligations. If creditors lost this confidence, the federal government's interest costs would likely increase substantially and there would likely be broader disruptions to financial markets.

On April 25, 2011, the Treasury Borrowing Advisory Committee, a group of senior representatives from investment funds and banks that presents their observations on the overall strength of the U.S. economy and provides recommendations on a variety of technical debt management issues to the Treasury Department, sent a letter to Secretary Geithner expressing its views on the impact on financial markets if the debt ceiling is not raised.[44] The letter warned that any delay by Treasury in making an interest or principal payment could trigger another "catastrophic financial crisis." Further, the committee described several potential consequences stemming from a Treasury default on its obligations including a downgrade of the U.S. credit rating, an increase in federal and private borrowing costs, damage to the economic recovery, and broader disruptions to the financial system. Finally, the committee also warned that a prolonged delay in raising the debt limit could have negative consequences on the market before the time when default would actually occur.[45]

Considerations for the Current Debt Limit Debate

There are various viewpoints about how to deal with the current debt limit issues. The debt subject to limit will generally continue to rise as long as the budget remains in deficit or trust funds remain in surplus. To avoid raising the debt limit and continue normal government operations, significant spending cuts and/or revenue increases would be required.

Views on the Debt Limit, Prioritization, and Default

Various members of the Obama Administration have stated that default can not be avoided if the debt limit is not raised and the consequences of a federal default would be serious. Treasury Secretary Geithner's letter of January 6, 2011, provided Treasury's views on the "consequences of default by the United States," describing, among other things, payments that would be "discontinued, limited, or adversely affected."[46] The letter also said a short-term or limited default on legal obligations would cause "catastrophic damage to the economy."[47] Chairman of the White House Council of Economic Advisers Austan Goolsbee elaborated, saying that a default would cause "a worse financial economic crisis than anything we saw in 2008."[48] Secretary Geithner, in his letter to Congress added, "Default would have prolonged and far-reaching negative consequences on the safe-haven status of Treasuries and the dollar's dominant role in the international financial system, causing further increases in interest rates and reducing the willingness of investors here and around the world to invest in the United States."[49] In a later online posting, Treasury Deputy Secretary Neal Wolin wrote that proposals to prioritize payments on the national debt above other legal obligations would not prevent default and would bring the same economic consequences Secretary Geithner described.[50] Looking forward, Secretary Geithner said in his letter that in addition to addressing the debt limit, the President wants to work with Congress to address the federal government's fiscal position with particular attention to addressing "medium- and long-term fiscal challenges."[51]

Other policy makers have expressed some contrasting perspectives focusing on the need to tie proposals to raise the debt limit to spending cuts, changes to the budget process, or instructions on how to deal with the payment of obligations if the debt limit is reached. For example, Senator Jim DeMint wrote in an op-ed that a vote to raise the debt limit should be opposed "unless Congress first passes a balanced-budget amendment that requires a two-thirds majority to raise taxes."[52] Other proposals also have emerged. Senator Pat Toomey and Representative Tom McClintock introduced legislation that, in the event of a debt limit crisis, would require Treasury to make payment of principal and interest on debt held by the public a higher priority than all other federal government obligations (S. 163/H.R. 421; 112th Congress). In a letter to Secretary Geithner, Senator Toomey said "This legislation is designed to maintain orderly financial markets by reassuring investors in U.S. Treasury securities that their investments are perfectly safe even in the unlikely event that the debt limit is temporarily reached."[53] Similarly, Senator David Vitter and Representative Dean Heller introduced legislation that would require priority be given to payment of all obligations on the debt held by the public and Social Security benefits in the event that the debt limit is reached (S. 259/H.R. 568; 112th Congress).[54] Representative Marlin Stutzman introduced legislation that would require priority be given to payment of all obligations on the debt held by the public, Social Security benefits, and specified military expenditures in the event that the debt limit is reached (H.R. 728; 112th Congress).[55]

Proposals have been introduced in both the House and the Senate to include various budgetary controls to accompany an increase in the debt limit. In the House, Speaker Boehner introduced the Budget Control Act of 2011 (House Substitute Amendment to S. 627) on July 25, 2011. In this legislation, limits on discretionary spending would be put into place through the use of discretionary spending caps over the next 10 years (from FY2012-FY2021), enforced by automatic spending reductions, referred to as a sequester, of non-exempt spending if the caps are breached. The legislation also requires a vote on a Balanced Budget Amendment,[56] the creation of a Joint Committee on Deficit Reduction, and various changes to the student loan program. The debt limit can be increased by up to $2.5 trillion in three stages subject to specific notification requirements of the President and a Congressional vote on a resolution of disapproval.

In the Senate, Majority Leader Harry Reid introduced a different measure also titled Budget Control Act of 2011 (S.Amdt. 581 to S. 1323) on July 25, 2011. In this measure, separate caps on discretionary spending are put into place for the security and non-security categories through FY2014 and then a general cap on discretionary spending through FY2021. These caps are also enforced by a sequester of non-exempt spending if the caps are breached. Spending cuts are achieved through the auction of spectrum licenses, changes to the student loan program, and reductions in certain agricultural programs. Like the House measure, this bill also contains a provision that would create a Joint Committee on Deficit Reduction. The debt limit would be increased by $2.7 trillion upon the enactment of this measure.

Economists have expressed concern regarding the current level of federal debt. However, they maintain that there would be significant consequences if the debt limit is not raised. Federal Reserve Chairman Ben Bernanke has stated that Congress must work to put a plan in to place that would lower the nation's federal debt. He also stated that not raising the debt limit could ultimately lead the nation to default on its debt with catastrophic implications for the financial system and the economy.[57] Mark Zandi, chief economist for Moody's Analytics, expressed similar sentiments regarding the debt limit and the potential impact on the economy. He stated, "Global investors are already anxious regarding our ability to come to a political consensus to address the nation's fiscal challenges; a protracted debate over the debt ceiling would be very counterproductive."[58] Donald Marron, the director of the Urban-Brookings Tax Policy Center and a former acting director of the Congressional Budget Office, recently expressed similar views. He stated, "Geithner is correct that the debt limit must increase. With monthly deficits running more than $100 billion, it's simply unthinkable that Congress could cut spending or increase revenue enough to avoid borrowing more.... Still, I am troubled by any suggestion that the United States might willingly default on its public debt. Doing so would have absolutely no upside."[59]

Questions have been raised regarding what constitutes a legal "default" by the government. Some proponents of a prioritization system suggest that the term "default" applies only if the government fails to pay interest on debt obligations held by third parties. Opponents of prioritization appear to argue that the term "default" applies not only to a failure to pay third-party debt holders, but also to the failure by the government to meet any obligation authorized by law, which would include a failure to fund an appropriated program, pay federal salaries or benefits, or pay an amount owed on a federal contract. No general statutory definition of the term "default" exists; however, *Black's Law Dictionary* 428 (7th Ed. 1999) defines the term "default" as "the failure to make a payment when due," which, if accepted as the governing definition, would not appear to distinguish between various types of government obligations.

Aside from technical definitions, financial markets' perceptions of what constitutes a default, or a real threat of default, may be more significant when assessing the potential impacts of not raising the debt limit. For example, if the federal government were to prioritize payments on debt obligations above other obligations, it is not clear whether financial markets would find this distinction to be significant when deciding whether and how to invest in federal government Treasury securities, since Treasury would be postponing payments on other legal obligations. Because perceptions such as these are difficult if not impossible to predict, it is not clear what the effects of prioritization would be, in the event of an impasse.[60]

Can an Increase in the Current Debt Limit be Avoided?

Under current estimates, the federal government will have to issue an additional $738 billion in debt on net above the current statutory limit to finance all obligations for the second half of FY2011.[61] If the debt limit is reached and Treasury is no longer able to issue federal debt, federal spending would have to be decreased or federal revenues would have to be increased by a corresponding amount to cover the gap in what cannot be borrowed. To put this into context, the federal government is expected to spend roughly $688 billion on discretionary programs and $1,054 billion on mandatory programs in the second half of FY2011.[62] If the debt limit were not raised and all discretionary spending in the second half of the fiscal year were eliminated, the federal government would still have to find further savings to cover its borrowing needs. Alternatively, the federal government would be able to cover its borrowing needs by cutting nearly 70% of outlays for mandatory programs in the second half of FY2011 (April through September 30, 2011).

In terms of revenues, the federal government is expected to collect roughly $1,114 billion in the second half of FY2011 (April through September 30, 2011). To cover the $738 billion in borrowing needs solely by increasing revenues, the government would have to raise taxes by about two-thirds. These spending cuts and revenue increases provide an approximation of what would be required to cover the borrowing need for the remainder of FY2011 under current policy. They do not address what would be required in FY2012 and beyond to avoid having to raise the debt limit.

How Much Should the Debt Limit Be Raised?

Under current policy, the debt subject to limit is projected to increase throughout the remainder of the decade. The debt subject to limit is projected to reach $15,032 billion at the end of FY2011.[63] Under President Obama's FY2012 budget proposals, it is projected to reach $26,346 billion at the end of FY2021.[64] This represents an increase of $1 trillion in each fiscal year during the FY2011 to FY2021 period. Increases in debt subject to limit at this level occur even as the budget deficit is projected to decline, in nominal dollars, between FY2012 and FY2015. Between FY2016 and FY2019, the budget deficit is projected to remain roughly stable, before rising thereafter.[65] In other words, the debt subject to limit increases even if the budget deficit declines in nominal terms as issuing debt would still be required to finance federal spending in excess of federal revenues (i.e., budget deficits).

According to the figures provided in the House Budget Committee report (H.Rept. 112-58) accompanying the House FY2012 Budget Resolution (H.Con.Res. 34) agreed to on April 15, 2011, the debt subject to limit is projected to rise from $16,204 billion at the end of FY2012 to $23,105 billion at the end of FY2021. This means that if the policies contained in the House-passed budget resolution are enacted, the debt limit would have to increase by $6,901 billion (or roughly $800 billion in each fiscal year) during the FY2012 to FY2021 period.

Given the borrowing requirements under both the President's FY2012 budget and the House- passed budget resolution, the current estimates stipulate the increases in the debt limit that would be required. However, depending on the spending and revenue proposals that may be subsequently enacted, borrowing requirements could change going forward. These borrowing requirements will dictate the level of debt and subsequent future increases in the debt limit. How often Congress wishes to reconsider statutory debt limit legislation typically affects the level at which the debt limit is set.

Temporary increases in the debt limit have been used in the past to provide additional time for Congress to consider debt limit increases. However, past temporary debt limit increases were eventually followed by permanent increases. If a temporary increase were to expire and the debt limit were to revert to a prior lower level, Congress may want to enact legislation that would result in a budget surplus in excess of the intragovernmental surplus in order to lower the level of debt subject to limit. If this legislation is not enacted and fully realized prior to the expiration of the temporary limit, then the level of debt would exceed the lowered debt limit.

IMPLICATIONS OF FUTURE FEDERAL DEBT ON THE DEBT LIMIT

It is extremely difficult for Congress to effectively influence short-term fiscal and budgetary policy through action on legislation adjusting the debt limit. For example, the debt is projected to reach the current limit after spending and revenue decisions for half of the current fiscal year have already been made. The need to raise (or lower) the limit during a session of Congress is driven by previous decisions regarding revenues and spending. These decisions stem from legislation enacted earlier in the session or in prior years.

From the Congressional Budget Office (CBO):

> By itself, setting a limit on the debt is an ineffective means of controlling deficits because the decisions that necessitate borrowing are made through other legislative actions. By the time an increase in the debt ceiling comes up for approval, it is too late to avoid paying the government's pending bills without incurring serious negative consequences.[66]

Nevertheless, the consideration of debt limit legislation often is viewed as an opportunity to reexamine fiscal and budgetary policy. Consequently, House and Senate action on legislation adjusting the debt limit often is complicated, hindered by policy disagreements, and subject to delay.[67] Many in Congress have stated that the debt limit should not be raised without accompanying deficit reduction legislation.

Generally, the following scenarios dictate whether or not an increase in the debt limit would be necessary, all else constant:

- If the federal budget is in deficit and intragovernmental debt is rising, an increase in the debt limit would be necessary.
- If the federal budget is in deficit and intragovernmental debt falls by an amount that is smaller than the budget deficit, an increase in the debt limit would be necessary.
- If the federal budget is balanced or in surplus and intragovernmental debt rises by an amount that is larger than the budget surplus, an increase in the debt limit would be necessary.
- If the federal budget is balanced or in surplus and intragovernmental debt is falling, an increase in the debt limit would not be required.

In other words, increases in the statutory debt limit would be required if the budget remains in deficit, even if future deficit levels are lower than they are at present, or if there are increases in the level of intragovernmental debt. If intragovernmental debt is declining, presumably due to the need of certain trust funds to redeem their holdings of Treasury securities in order to pay benefits, the Treasury would have to provide the trust funds with cash either from the General Fund resources or by issuing additional debt to the public to raise cash. If the federal budget is in deficit, Treasury would have to raise the necessary cash to redeem trust fund securities by issuing debt to the public. This would not require an increase in the debt limit, as the decline in intragovernmental debt would be offset by an equal increase in debt held by the public. A decline in intragovernmental debt as a result of a redemption in trust fund securities could be financed by using surplus cash if the federal budget is in surplus at that time.[68] In this situation, debt held by the public debt, debt held by government accounts, and total federal debt would decrease. If the budget surplus were less than the reduction in intragovernmental debt, the increase in the debt held by the public would be offset by the decline in intragovernmental debt, resulting in a decrease in the total debt.

APPENDIX. DETAILED HISTORY ON PAST TREASURY ACTIONS DURING PREVIOUS DEBT LIMIT CRISES

Selected Actions in 1985

In September 1985, the Treasury Department informed Congress that it had reached the statutory debt limit. As a result, Treasury had to take extraordinary measures to meet the government's cash requirements. Treasury used various internal transactions involving the Federal Financing Bank (FFB) and delayed public auctions of government debt. It also was unable to issue, or had to delay issuing, new short-term government securities to the Civil Service Retirement and Disability Trust Fund, the Social Security Trust Funds, and several smaller trust funds. Issuing new government securities to the trust funds would have caused the federal debt to exceed the debt limit. During this period, the bulk of Social Security payroll tax revenues were kept in a non-interest bearing account.

Treasury took the additional step of "disinvesting" the Civil Service Retirement and Disability Trust Fund, the Social Security Trust Funds, and several smaller trust funds by redeeming some trust fund securities earlier than usual. Premature redemption of these securities created room under the debt ceiling for Treasury to borrow sufficient cash from the public to pay other obligations, including November Social Security benefits.[69]

As a result of these various actions, Social Security benefit payments and other federal payments were not jeopardized. The debt limit was subsequently temporarily increased on November 14, 1985 (P.L. 99-155) and permanently increased on December 12, 1985 (P.L. 99-177) from $1,824 billion to $2,079 billion. Both P.L. 99-155 and P.L. 99-177 included provisions to require the Treasury to restore any interest income lost to the trust funds as a result of delayed investments and early redemptions.

Concerning the Treasury's management of the Social Security Trust Funds during the 1985 debt limit impasse, the General Accounting Office (GAO, now the Government Accountability Office) wrote: "We conclude that, although some of the Secretary's actions appear in retrospect to have been in violation of the requirements of the Social Security Act, we cannot say that the Secretary acted unreasonably given the extraordinary situation in which he was operating."[70] In particular, GAO found that not all the delayed investment and securities redemptions during the period from September through November 1985 were necessary to meet Social Security benefit payments, and the excess was used to finance general government operations.[71]

Following the 1985 debt limit crisis, Congress formally authorized the Secretary of the Treasury to declare a debt issuance suspension period and, during such periods, to depart from normal trust fund investment practices with respect to certain funds such as the Civil Service Retirement and Disability Fund and the TSP's G Fund (P.L. 99-509, the Omnibus Budget Reconciliation Act of 1986). Funds raised by procedures authorized during a debt issuance suspension period can only be used to the extent necessary to prevent the public debt from exceeding the debt limit. After the debt issuance suspension period has ended, P.L. 99-509 requires Treasury to make the trust funds whole by issuing the appropriate amount of securities and crediting any interest lost due to non-investment or early disinvestment of these funds.[72] Such authority to depart from normal trust fund investment practices was not provided with respect to the Social Security Trust Funds. A provision to allow such authority was dropped from P.L. 99-509 during conference.

Selected Actions in 1995-1996

Following the enactment of this additional authority, the first debt issuance suspension period was announced on November 15, 1995. Treasury, once again, used non-traditional methods of financing, including some of the methods used during the 1985 crisis as well as not reinvesting some of the maturing Treasury securities held by the Exchange Stabilization Fund.[73] In addition, Treasury utilized the new authority that was enacted under P.L. 99-509 to declare a debt issuance suspension period.

In early 1996, Treasury announced that it had insufficient cash to pay Social Security benefits for March 1996.[74] Congress responded on February 1, 1996, by passing P.L. 104-103, which provided the Treasury with temporary authority to issue securities to the public in an amount equal to the March 1996 Social Security benefit payments. Treasury issued about $29 billion of securities on February 23, 1996, and, under P.L. 104-103, these new securities were not to count against the debt limit until March 15, 1996. On March 7, 1996, Congress passed P.L. 104-115, which amended P.L. 104-103 to permit Treasury to continue investing payroll tax revenues in government securities and also to extend the exemption of the securities issued under P.L. 104- 103 from counting against the debt limit until March 30, 1996.

The debt limit was permanently increased on March 29, 1996 (P.L. 104-121) from $4,900 billion to $5,500 billion. P.L. 104-121 also codified Congress's understanding that the Secretary of the Treasury and other federal officials are not authorized to use Social Security and Medicare funds for debt management purposes.[75] SSA states the following:

> Specifically, the Secretary of the Treasury and other federal officials are required not to delay or otherwise underinvest incoming receipts to the Social Security and Medicare Trust Funds. They are also required not to sell, redeem, or otherwise disinvest securities, obligations, or other assets of these Trust Funds except when necessary to provide for the payment of benefits and administrative expenses of the programs.[76]

These restrictions apply to the Federal Old-Age and Survivors Insurance (OASI) Trust Fund, the Federal Disability Insurance (DI) Trust Fund, the Federal Hospital Insurance (HI) Trust Fund, and the Federal Supplementary Medical Insurance (SMI) Trust Fund.

Social Security Trust Fund Cash and Investment Management Practices

By law, the Social Security Trust Funds must be invested in interest-bearing obligations of the United States or in obligations guaranteed as to both principal and interest by the United States (42 U.S.C. § 401(d) and 42 U.S.C. § 1320b-15).[77] The securities that the Treasury issues to the Social Security Trust Funds count toward the federal debt limit.

Under normal procedures, Social Security revenues (Social Security payroll taxes and individual income taxes) are immediately credited to the Social Security Trust Funds in the form of short-term, non-marketable Treasury securities called certificates of indebtedness (CIs). Under the terms of this exchange, when Treasury credits payroll tax and other revenues to Social Security in the form of CIs, the revenues themselves become available in the General Fund for other government operations.

CIs generally mature on the following June 30. Each June 30, any surplus for the year is converted from short-term Treasury securities to long-term, non-marketable Treasury securities called "special-issue obligations" or "specials."[78] In addition, other special issues that have just matured and that are not needed to pay near-term benefits are reinvested in special-issue obligations. Interest income is credited to the trust funds semi-annually (on June 30 and December 31) in the form of additional special-issue obligations.[79]

Social Security benefits are paid by the Treasury from the General Fund. When Treasury pays Social Security benefits, it redeems an equivalent amount of Treasury securities held by the trust funds in order to reimburse the General Fund.

In 2011, when the federal government is expected to reach the current debt ceiling, the Social Security program is projected to run a cash deficit. That is, Social Security's tax revenues are projected to be less than outlays for benefit payments and administration.[80] In a year when Social Security runs a cash flow deficit, the Treasury redeems some long-term government securities held by the trust funds. However, Social Security will still need to invest in non-marketable, short-term government securities in 2011 to manage short-term cash flows during the periods between receiving revenues and paying benefits (42 U.S.C. § 401(a), 42 U.S.C. § 401(d) and 42 U.S.C. § 1320b-15). Investing the trust funds' revenues for even very short periods ensures that the trust funds maximize their interest earnings. Social Security will also need to invest in non-marketable, long-term government securities in June 2011 when short-term and certain long-term trust fund securities mature and amounts not needed to pay near-term benefits are rolled over into long-term government securities, and in June and December 2011 when semi-annual interest income is paid in the form of government securities.

In addition, Social Security will draw on general revenues as a result of the Tax Relief, Unemployment Insurance Reauthorization, and Job Creation Act of 2010 (P.L. 111-312, signed on December 17, 2010). Among other provisions, P.L. 111-312 provides a temporary 2 percentage point reduction in the Social Security payroll tax for employees and the self-employed in 2011, resulting in a tax rate of 4.2% for employees and 10.4% for the self-employed.[81] To protect the Social Security Trust Funds from a loss of payroll tax revenues, P.L. 111-312 appropriates to the Social Security Trust Funds amounts equal to the reduction in payroll tax revenues. The law specifies that these appropriated amounts "shall be transferred from the General Fund at such times and in such manner as to replicate to the extent possible the transfers which would have occurred to such Trust Fund had such amendments not been enacted."[82]

Depending on the extent and duration of any future debt limit crisis, and also on Treasury prioritization decisions, Social Security trust fund investment management procedures and benefit payments potentially could be affected because of the requirement that Treasury obligations cannot be issued to the Social Security trust funds if doing so would exceed the debt limit.[83] At the same time, as described above, P.L. 104-121 restricts the Treasury Secretary's ability to delay or otherwise underinvest incoming receipts to the Social Security and Medicare Trust Funds. Delayed issuance of government obligations to the trust funds, or early redemption of some trust fund assets, could accelerate depletion of the trust funds and move up the expected insolvency date, absent congressional action to make the trust funds whole.

Depending on the government's cash position in a given month, Treasury may need to issue new public debt to raise the cash needed to pay benefits. Treasury may be unable to issue new public debt, however, if doing so would exceed the debt limit. Social Security benefit payments may be delayed or jeopardized if the Treasury does not have enough cash on hand to pay benefits.

ACKNOWLEDGMENTS

The authors wish to thank D. Andrew Austin, Marc Labonte, and Todd B. Tatelman for their helpful comments on this report.

End Notes

[1] The statutory debt limit may be compared with the current level of "debt subject to limit" in U.S. Department of the Treasury, *Daily Treasury Statement*, Table III-C, available at http://fms.treas.gov/dts/index.html.

[2] Letter from Timothy F. Geithner, Secretary of the Treasury, to the Hon. Harry Reid, Senate majority leader, January 6, 2011, available at http://www.treasury.gov/connect/blog/

Pages/letter.aspx (hereafter Treasury January 6th letter). U.S. Department of the Treasury, *Treasury Assistant Secretary for Financial Markets Mary Miller February 2011 Quarterly Refunding Statement*, February 2, 2011, available at http://www.treasury.gov/press-center/press-releases/Pages/tg1045.aspx. Letter from Timothy F. Geithner, Secretary of the Treasury, to the Hon. John A. Boehner, Speaker of the House, May 2, 2011, available at http://www.treasury.gov/connect/blog/Documents/ FINAL%20Debt%20Limit%20Letter%2005-02-2011%20Boehner.pdf (hereafter Treasury May 2nd letter).

[3] Treasury May 2nd letter and Letter from Timothy F. Geithner, Secretary of the Treasury, to the Hon. Harry Reid, Senate Majority Leader, May 16, 2011, available at http://www.treasury.gov/connect/blog/Documents/20110516Letter%20to%20Congress.pdf (hereafter Treasury May 16th letter).

[4] The possible scenario sometimes has been referred to generically as a debt limit crisis. U.S. General Accounting Office (now the Government Accountability Office and hereafter GAO), *Debt Ceiling: Analysis of Actions During the 2003 Debt Issuance Suspension Periods*, GAO-04-526, May 2004.

[5] This section draws on CRS Report 98-453, *Debt-Limit Legislation in the Congressional Budget Process*, by Bill Heniff Jr., and CRS Report RL31967, *The Debt Limit: History and Recent Increases*, by D. Andrew Austin and Mindy R. Levit.

[6] If the budget is in surplus and intragovernmental debt rises by an amount that is less than the budget surplus, the total debt would not increase. See the later discussion in the section titled "Implications of Future Federal Debt on the Debt Limit."

[7] GAO, *Federal Trust and Other Earmarked Funds Answers to Frequently Asked Questions*, GAO-01-199SP, January 2001, pp. 17-18.

[8] For an explanation of how this process works for the Social Security trust funds, see *Appendix.*

[9] Chapter 56, 40 Stat. 288 (1917). The debt limit is now codified at 31 U.S.C. § 3101.

[10] The Treasury defines "Total Public Debt Subject to Limit" as "the Total Public Debt Outstanding less Unamortized Discount on Treasury Bills and Zero-Coupon Treasury Bonds, old debt issued prior to 1917, and old currency called United States Notes, as well as Debt held by the Federal Financing Bank and Guaranteed Debt." Approximately 0.5% of total federal debt is not subject to the debt limit. For more information, see U.S. Office of Management and Budget (hereafter OMB), *Budget of the U.S. Government, Analytical Perspectives*, Chapter 6 and Table 6-2.

[11] *See generally,* 31 U.S.C. §§ 3321 *et seq.* for the Treasury Secretary's duty to pay obligations. Regarding trust fund investments, see, for example, 42 U.S.C. § 401 (Social Security Trust Funds) and 5 U.S.C. § 8348 (Civil Service Retirement and Disability Trust Fund). The debt limit is codified at 31 U.S.C. § 3101.

[12] For example, see archived CRS Report 95-1109, *Authority to Tap Trust Funds and Establish Payment Priorities if the Debt Limit is not Increased*, by Thomas J. Nicola and Morton Rosenberg (available from CRS upon request).

[13] Congress formally authorized the additional powers to the Treasury Secretary under a "debt issuance suspension period" in the Omnibus Budget Reconciliation Act of 1986 (P.L. 99-509) and Thrift Savings Fund Investment Act of 1987 (P.L. 100-43).

[14] Treasury May 16th letter.

[15] For a more detailed analysis of past Treasury actions surrounding the debt limit impasses of 1985 and 1995-1996, see the *Appendix.*

[16] Treasury also redeemed some of the Social Security Trust Funds' holdings of long-term securities to reimburse the General Fund for cash payments of benefits in September

through November 1985. As described above, during this period, the Treasury was unable to follow its normal procedure of issuing short-term securities to the trust funds and then redeeming short-term securities to reimburse the General Fund when it paid Social Security benefits.

[17] Treasury's Exchange Stabilization Fund buys and sells foreign currency to promote exchange rate stability and counter disorderly conditions in the foreign exchange market.

[18] As described in the *Appendix,* under normal procedures Treasury pays Social Security benefits from the General Fund and offsets this by redeeming an equivalent amount of the trust funds' holdings of government debt. In order to pay Social Security benefits, and depending on the government's cash position at the time, Treasury may need to issue new public debt to raise the cash needed to pay benefits. Treasury may be unable to issue new public debt, however, because of the debt limit. Social Security benefit payments may be delayed or jeopardized if the Treasury does not have enough cash on hand to pay benefits.

[19] Federal Reserve Bank, "Factors Affecting Reserve Balances", Table 8, April 21, 2011, available at http://www.federalreserve.gov/releases/h41/hist/h41hist8.pdf.

[20] For a discussion of how Treasury's cash management practices and borrowing costs were affected during previous debt limit event periods, see GAO, *Delays Create Debt Management Challenges and Increase Uncertainty in the Treasury Market*, GAO-11-203, February 2011, pp. 10-18.

[21] Treasury January 6th letter.

[22] Letter from Timothy F. Geithner, Secretary of the Treasury, to the Hon. Harry Reid, Senate majority leader, April 4, 2011, available at http://www.treasury.gov/connect/blog/Documents/FINAL%20Letter%2004-04-2011%20Reid%20Debt%20Limit.pdf.

[23] Treasury May 2nd letter.

[24] For more information, see CRS Report R41811, *State and Local Government Series (SLGS) Treasury Debt: A Description*, by Steven Maguire.

[25] Treasury May 16th letter.

[26] A more in-depth discussion of these proposals and their implications can be found in the section titled "Views on the Debt Limit, Prioritization, and Default."

[27] U.S. Congress, Senate Committee on Finance, *Increase of Permanent Public Debt Limit*, S.Rpt. 99-144, September 26, 1985. For more information, see archived CRS Report 95-1109, *Authority to Tap Trust Funds and Establish Payment Priorities if the Debt Limit is Not Increased*, by Thomas J. Nicola and Morton Rosenberg (available from CRS upon request).

[28] "Treasury: Proposals to 'Prioritize' Payments on U.S. Debt Not Workable: Would Not Prevent Default," Neal Wolin, Deputy Secretary of the Treasury, January 21, 2011, at http://www.treasury.gov/connect/blog/Pages/Proposals-to-Prioritize-Payments-on-US-Debt-Not-Workable-Would-Not-Prevent-Default.aspx.

[29] Letter from GAO to the Hon. Bob Packwood, chairman of Senate Finance Committee, GAO B-138524, October 9, 1985, at http://redbook.gao.gov/14/fl0065142.php.

[30] While CRS has not located a list of established priorities to pay bills during a lapse in increasing the debt limit, OMB previously prepared a list of excepted functions that the government should continue to conduct during a government shutdown caused by a lapse in enacting appropriations. These priorities are based on a distinction between functions deemed excepted, such as providing health care or air traffic control, and those deemed non-excepted. If it should become necessary to establish priorities to pay bills when the debt limit has not been increased, it is possible that the Secretary of the Treasury may look to this

list of essential functions for some guidance. See later discussion in the section titled "Distinction Between a Debt Limit Crisis and a Government Shutdown."

[31] 31 U.S.C. § 1512, a provision of the Antideficiency Act, for example, states that appropriations for a definite period must be apportioned by such things as months, activities, or a combination of them to avoid obligation at a rate that would indicate a necessity of a deficiency or supplemental appropriations for the period. While apportionment commonly is used to control the rate at which agencies are allowed to *obligate* funds such as by placing orders and signing contracts, the text of Section 1512 also provides that it may be used to avoid *expending* funds.

[32] 2 U.S.C. §§ 681-692. During the period leading up to enactment of the Impoundment Control Act of 1974, the Nixon Administration used apportionment authority as a tool ultimately to limit outlays to conform to the President's budgetary priorities. Several lawsuits were brought to challenge the President's authority not to expend funds that Congress had appropriated and some lower courts held that the President lacked this authority. The Supreme Court did not address the merits of this issue.

[33] Generally, funds that have been proposed for deferral or rescission must be withheld for 45 days of continuous legislative session (excluding periods of more than three days when Congress is not in session), after which period they must be released unless Congress enacts a joint resolution to acquiesce in whole or in part to these requests. Congress sometimes responds to presidential deferral or rescission requests by acting on bills to defer or rescind different budget authorities from the ones that the President has proposed. Because deferrals or rescissions proposed by the President do not take effect unless Congress acquiesces to them, Congress as a matter of law has the final say on these matters. In practice, however, funds that are subject to these presidential requests often are withheld for long periods. For more information, see CRS Report RL33869, *Rescission Actions Since 1974: Review and Assessment of the Record*, by Virginia A. McMurtry.

[34] Discretionary spending is provided in, and controlled by, annual appropriations acts, which fund many of the routine activities commonly associated with such federal government functions as running executive branch agencies, congressional offices and agencies, and international operations of the government. Mandatory spending includes federal government spending on entitlement programs as well as other budget outlays controlled by laws other than appropriations acts. Mandatory spending also includes appropriated entitlements, such as Medicaid and certain veterans' programs, which are funded in annual appropriations acts. For more information, see CRS Report RS20129, *Entitlements and Appropriated Entitlements in the Federal Budget Process*, by Bill Heniff Jr.

[35] For example, because federal, state, and local government finances are linked by various intergovernmental transfers, late payment or nonpayment of federal obligations to states could affect the budgets and finances of local governments, such as school districts, counties, and municipalities.

[36] 31 U.S.C. § 3902.

[37] 26 U.S.C. § 6611.

[38] For information about the balances of all federal trust funds, see CRS Report R41328, *Federal Trust Funds and the Budget*, by Thomas L. Hungerford.

[39] Congressional Budget Office (hereafter, CBO), *The Economic and Budget Outlook: An Update*, August 1995, p. 49.

[40] In the event of a funding hiatus, the Antideficiency Act nevertheless allows an exception for agencies to incur obligations for emergencies involving the safety of human life or the

protection of property. For discussion, see CRS Report RL34680, *Shutdown of the Federal Government: Causes, Processes, and Effects*, by Clinton T. Brass.

[41] While this passage indicates that a delay in increasing the debt limit has the potential to postpone the payment of Social Security benefits, among other benefits, Social Security benefits have been paid on time during past debt limit crises. Non-marketable securities can be redeemed on demand. GAO, *A New Approach to the Public Debt Legislation Should be Considered*, FGMSD-79-58, September 1979, pp. 17-18, http://archive.gao.gov/f0302/110373.pdf.

[42] Ibid.

[43] GDP = consumption + investment + government spending + (exports – imports). If government spending declines, then GDP will also decline by definition, all else equal.

[44] More information on the Treasury Borrowing Advisory Committee can be found at http://www.treasury.gov/resource-center/data-chart-center/quarterly-refunding/Pages/default.aspx.

[45] Letter from Matthew E. Zames, Chairman of Treasury Borrowing Advisory Committee, to Timothy F. Geithner, April 25, 2011, available at http://www.sifma.org/issues/item.aspx?id=25013.

[46] Letter from Timothy F. Geithner, Secretary of the Treasury, to the Hon. Harry Reid, Senate majority leader, January 6, 2011, p. 4.

[47] Ibid., pp. 1, 3.

[48] ABC News *This Week*, Transcript: White House Adviser Austan Goolsbee, January 2, 2011, at http://abcnews.go.com/ThisWeek/week-transcript-white-house-adviser-austan-goolsbee/story?id=12522822.

[49] Treasury Secretary Geithner letter, January 6, 2011, p. 4.

[50] Neal Wolin, Deputy Secretary of the Treasury, "Treasury: Proposals to 'Prioritize' Payments on U.S. Debt Not Workable; Would Not Prevent Default," January 21, 2011, at http://www.treasury.gov/connect/blog/Pages/Proposalsto-Prioritize-Payments-on-US-Debt-Not-Workable-Would-Not-Prevent-Default.aspx.

[51] Treasury Secretary Geithner letter, January 6, 2011, p. 4.

[52] Senator Jim DeMint, "More Spending is a Threat to America," *Politico*, January 24, 2011, at http://www.politico.com/news/stories/0111/48020.html.

[53] Senator Pat Toomey, "Senator Toomey Sends Letter to Secretary Geithner on the Debt Limit," press release, February 2, 2011, http://toomey.senate.gov/record.cfm?id=330828&.

[54] Representative Dean Heller was sworn in to the U.S. Senate on May 9, 2011, to fill the seat of former Senator John Ensign who had resigned.

[55] These are examples of legislation introduced as of February 15, 2011. Some of this legislation has been considered as amendments to other legislation and were tabled or withdrawn. This is not intended to be a legislative tracking report.

[56] For more information on balanced budget amendments, see CRS Report R41907, *A Balanced Budget Constitutional Amendment: Background and Congressional Options* , by James V. Saturno and Megan Suzanne Lynch.

[57] Davidson, Paul, "Economy still in a deep hole, Bernanke says," USA Today, February 4, 2011.

[58] U.S. Congress, Senate Committee on the Budget, *Challenges for the U.S. Economic Recovery*, Testimony of Mark Zandi, February 3, 2011, available at http://budget.senate.gov/democratic/testimony/2011/Zandi_Senate_Budget_2_3_2011.pdf.

[59] Marron, Donald, "Debt Ceiling: Geithner Won't Let Us Default," *CNNMoney.com*, January 19, 2011.

[60] The potential effects of reaching the debt limit on financial markets are further discussed in the section titled "Potential Economic and Financial Effects."

[61] CRS calculations based on U.S. Congressional Budget Office, *The Budget and Economic Outlook: Fiscal Years 2011 to 2021*, January 2011, Tables 1-4 and C-2.

[62] Since January, Congress has provided full year appropriations for FY2011 (P.L. 112-10). However, the levels provided do not result in a significant change in discretionary outlays for FY2011.

[63] U.S. Congressional Budget Office, *The Budget and Economic Outlook: Fiscal Years 2011 to 2021*, January 2011, Table C-2.

[64] Office of Management and Budget, *Budget of the U.S. Government, Fiscal Year 2012, The Budget*, Table S-14, available at http://www.whitehouse.gov/sites/default/files/omb/budget/fy2012/assets/tables.pdf.

[65] Office of Management and Budget, *Budget of the U.S. Government, Fiscal Year 2012, The Budget*, Table S-1.

[66] U.S. Congressional Budget Office, *Federal Debt and Interest Costs*, December 2010, p. 23, available at http://www.cbo.gov/ftpdocs/119xx/doc11999/12-14-FederalDebt.pdf.

[67] For more information, see CRS Report RS21519, *Legislative Procedures for Adjusting the Public Debt Limit: A Brief Overview*, by Bill Heniff Jr.

[68] Under the most recent projections, the federal budget is expected to remain in deficit through FY2021 under current law. U.S. Congressional Budget Office, *The Budget and Economic Outlook: Fiscal Years 2011 to 2021*, January 2011, Table 1-1.

[69] Treasury redeemed some of the Social Security Trust Funds' holdings of long-term securities to reimburse the General Fund for cash payments of benefits in September through November 1985. As described above, during this period, the Treasury was unable to follow its normal procedure of issuing short-term securities to the trust funds and then redeeming short-term securities to reimburse the General Fund when it paid Social Security benefits.

[70] Letter from Charles A. Bowsher, Comptroller General of the United States, to the Hon. James R. Jones, chairman, Subcommittee on Social Security, House Committee on Ways and Means, December 5, 1985, GAO B-221077.2, http://archive.gao.gov/d12t3/128621.pdf.

[71] Ibid.

[72] GAO, *Debt Ceiling Options*, AIMD-96-20R, December 7, 1995, http://archive.gao.gov/paprpdf1/155750.pdf.

[73] Treasury's Exchange Stabilization Fund buys and sells foreign currency to promote exchange rate stability and counter disorderly conditions in the foreign exchange market.

[74] As described in later in this *Appendix*, under normal procedures Treasury pays Social Security benefits from the General Fund and offsets this by redeeming an equivalent amount of the trust funds' holdings of government debt. In order to pay Social Security benefits, and depending on the government's cash position at the time, Treasury may need to issue new public debt to raise the cash needed to pay benefits. Treasury may be unable to issue new public debt, however, because of the debt limit. Social Security benefit payments may be delayed or jeopardized if the Treasury does not have enough cash on hand to pay benefits.

[75] See 42 U.S.C. § 1320b-15.

[76] U.S. Social Security Administration, "Program Legislation Enacted in Early 1996," *Social Security Bulletin*, vol. 59, no. 2, Summer 1996, p. 65, at http://www.ssa.gov/policy/docs/ssb/v59n2/index.html.

[77] There are two sources of Social Security revenues: (1) payroll taxes paid by workers and employers and (2) federal income taxes paid by some beneficiaries on a portion of their benefits. In addition, Social Security receives income from trust fund investments. Interest

income is paid to the trust funds as a credit from the General Fund to the trust funds, in the form of additional non-marketable government securities.

[78] The trust funds' long-term securities have maturities ranging from 1 to 15 years and normally mature in June of the applicable year.

[79] For a detailed discussion, see Social Security Administration, Office of the Chief Actuary, *Social Security Trust Fund Investment Policies and Practices*, Actuarial Note Number 142, January 1999, http://www.ssa.gov/OACT/NOTES/pdf_notes/note142.pdf (hereafter cited as SSA Actuarial Note Number 142).

[80] For SSA's projections of Social Security trust fund operations, see 2010 Annual Report of the Board of Board of Trustees of the Federal Old-Age and Survivors Insurance and Federal Disability Insurance Trust Funds, Washington, DC, August 5, 2010, p. 2, http://www.ssa.gov/OACT/TR/2010/tr2010.pdf. For projections from the Congressional Budget Office (CBO), see 2010 Long-Term Projections for Social Security: Additional Information, Washington, DC, October 2010, p. 1, http://www.cbo.gov/ftpdocs/119xx/doc11943/10-22-SocialSecurity_chartbook.pdf and Combined OASDI Trust Funds, March 2011 Baseline, at http://www.cbo.gov/budget /factsheets/2011b/OASDI-TrustFunds.pdf. Social Security's cash deficit will be offset by interest income for many years, with the result that Social Security will have a positive total trust fund balance until the trust funds are exhausted in 2037 (under the intermediate projections of the Social Security Board of Trustees) or 2039 (under the projections by CBO). Social Security benefits scheduled under current law can be paid in full as long as there is a positive balance in the trust funds.

[81] P.L. 111-312 makes no change to the Social Security payroll tax rate for employers (6.2%) or to the amount of wages and net self-employment income subject to the Social Security payroll tax ($106,800 in 2011).

[82] See P.L. 111-312, Title VI (Temporary Employee Payroll Tax Cut), at http://www.gpo.gov/fdsys/pkg/PLAW-111publ312/pdf/PLAW-111publ312.pdf.

[83] SSA Actuarial Note Number 142, p. 3.

INDEX

A

B

C

D

E

F

G

S

T

U

V

W

Y